TEACH
MATH
WITH THE Wii

Engage Your K–7 Students through Gaming Technology

Meghan Hearn
Matthew C. Winner

International Society for Technology in Education
EUGENE, OREGON • WASHINGTON, DC

TEACH MATH WITH THE Wii
Engage Your K–7 Students through Gaming Technology
Meghan Hearn and Matthew C. Winner

Director of Book Publishing: *Courtney Burkholder*
Acquisitions Editor: *Jeff V. Bolkan*
Production Editors: *Tina Wells, Lynda Gansel*
Production Coordinator: *Emily Reed*
Graphic Designer: *Signe Landin*
Copy Editor: *Cecelia Hagen*
Proofreader: *Ann Skaugset*
Book Design, Cover Design, and Production: *Kim McGovern*

Library of Congress Cataloging-in-Publication Data

Hearn, Meghan, author.
  Teach math with the Wii : engage your K-7 students through gaming
technology / Meghan Hearn, Matthew C. Winner. — First edition.
    pages cm
    ISBN 978-1-56484-334-0 (pbk.)
1. Games in mathematics education. 2. Nintendo Wii video games.
  3. Mathematics—Study and teaching (Elementary) 4. Mathematics—Study
and teaching (Early childhood)   I. Winner, Matthew C., author. II. Title.
    QA20.G35H43 2013
    372.7—dc
                                                              2013015254

First Edition
ISBN: 978-1-56484-334-0 (paperback)
ISBN: 978-1-56484-483-5 (e-book)
Printed in the United States of America

Cover art and inside book art: © iStockphoto.com/linearcurves; © Dreamstime.
com/Joywang225, Svetlana Gucalo, Agsandrew; *Avatar art:* © iStockphoto.com/
Electric_Crayon; authors' Miis (p. iv, p. v, p. 98, p. 105) created by the authors

Photographs: Libby Bartleson (p. 11, p. 12, p. 19)

ISTE* is a registered trademark of the International Society for Technology in Education.

About ISTE

The International Society for Technology in Education (ISTE) is the trusted source for professional development, knowledge generation, advocacy, and leadership for innovation. ISTE is the premier membership association for educators and education leaders engaged in improving teaching and learning by advancing the effective use of technology in PK–12 and teacher education.

Home to ISTE's annual conference and exposition and the widely adopted NETS, ISTE represents more than 100,000 professionals worldwide. We support our members with information, networking opportunities, and guidance as they face the challenge of transforming education. To find out more about these and other ISTE initiatives, visit our website at www.iste.org.

As part of our mission, ISTE Book Publishing works with experienced educators to develop and produce practical resources for classroom teachers, teacher educators, and technology leaders. Every manuscript we select for publication is carefully peer-reviewed and professionally edited. We value your feedback on this book and other ISTE products. Email us at books@iste.org.

International Society for Technology in Education
Washington, DC, Office:
    1710 Rhode Island Ave. NW, Suite 900
    Washington, DC 20036-3132
Eugene, Oregon, Office:
    180 West 8th Ave., Suite 300
    Eugene, OR 97401-2916
Order Desk: 1.800.336.5191
Order Fax: 1.541.302.3778
Customer Service: orders@iste.org
Book Publishing: books@iste.org
Book Sales and Marketing: booksmarketing@iste.org
Web: www.iste.org

About the Authors

Meg's Mii (Wii avatar)

Meghan (Meg) Hearn is a mathematics educator and specialist in the Howard County Public School System in Maryland. She facilitates school-based professional development with elementary school teachers focusing on developing conceptual understanding through problem-based teaching. Meg has contributed to a multitude of international, national, state, and local presentations and has presented virtually at the TL Virtual Cafe and with the Maryland Society for Educational Technology. She has been published in *School Library Journal* and is an adjunct faculty member at Notre Dame of Maryland University, where she teaches courses in mathematics education at the graduate level.

Meg holds a bachelor's degree from University of Maryland, a master's degree in education from McDaniel College, a post-master's certificate in administration and supervision from Johns Hopkins University, and is an Early Adolescent Mathematics National Board Certified Teacher. Meg also has experience as a primary and intermediate classroom teacher and grant project manager. She has a passion for using technology as a tool to encourage girls in mathematics and to engage all students in mathematics.

Matthew's Mii (Wii avatar)

Matthew C. Winner is a teacher librarian in the Howard County Public School System in Maryland. His library media program is aligned with ISTE's NETS for Teachers and the AASL Standards for the 21st-Century Learner. Before teaching in the elementary school library, Matthew taught in the fourth grade. He holds a bachelor's of science in elementary education from Towson University, a master's of science in school library media from McDaniel College, and is a National Board Certified Teacher in the area of library media.

Matthew has given presentations at conferences at the state, national, and international levels and has presented virtually at the TL Virtual Cafe. He has had articles published in *Knowledge Quest* and *School Library Journal,* and he is the author of the Busy Librarian blog. In 2012, Matthew was named Maryland Outstanding Educator Using Technology by the Maryland Society for Educational Technology. In 2013, he received ISTE's SIGMS Technology Innovation award. His love of video games and passion for teaching have earned him recognition as a 2013 *Library Journal* Mover & Shaker. He is also the cofounder of the Level Up Book Club, an online book club for teachers and professionals focused on game-based learning and gamification.

For more information on the Level Up Book Club, visit http://levelupbc.blogspot.com. Learn more about Matthew's library program and work at large at www.busylibrarian.com. Follow Matthew on Twitter at @MatthewWinner or email him directly at mwinne2@gmail.com.

Acknowledgments

My heartfelt thanks to Matthew for his dedication, creativity, and collaboration that helped make this idea a reality. —M.H.

My thanks and gratitude to Meg for knowing not only how to speak the standards, but for showing how to bring them to life. —M.W.

We would like to thank to our reviewers and editors at ISTE for their feedback and questions, which improved the landscape of this book. We offer enthusiastic cheers to our students, who allowed us to take instruction places they'd never expected and, in return, became our best advocates for teaching math with the Wii. And we thank our administrators and supervisors for their trust in our exploration of an unconventional tool to challenge the way we connect with our students.

Dedication

To my children, Taylor, Tierney, Riordan, and Ahnya who have taught me so much about how they learn mathematics and use technology, and to my husband, Adam, who encourages and supports all of my endeavors.

—Meghan

To my dad, for introducing me to the ways of Pong, the secrets of Adventure, the risks of Pitfall, and for playing with me, console after console.

—Matthew

Contents

Foreword

As educators, we all know how important it is to gain and sustain students' attention, and to engage their minds in meaningful ways to promote learning. However, did you know that engaging students' bodies during the process is also key to facilitating learning? We are finding that the ergonomics of traditional classrooms, with students sitting in chairs for significant periods of time, is actually antithetical to learning. Yet we continue to perpetuate such fallacies, maybe in part because we are not aware of useful alternatives.

Teach Math with the Wii offers a valuable resource for educators who are interested in breaking tradition by using video games to facilitate learning, and in using the Nintendo Wii to make learning active, both mentally and physically. Although you may not be familiar with research correlating physical activity with learning, I'm sure you've seen kids spending hours and hours fixated on playing video games. Maybe you, yourself, have reached "flow" state and played a video game for hours without realizing it. There's little doubt that video games and gaming technology can be very engaging, but can they be educational as well?

Although research on the effectiveness of game-based learning in K–12 settings has yielded mixed results, for the most part, studies indicate that playing video games can enhance student motivation and achievement, particularly if teachers do the right things before, during, and after gameplay. Meghan Hearn and Matthew Winner's book on teaching math with the Wii does just that: it provides practical guidelines and examples for what teachers should do to properly integrate the use of video games into their curriculum.

Many argue that today's youth are significantly different from prior generations. Some even suggest that they learn in fundamentally different ways. The jury is still out on these arguments, but the fact remains that kids today like to play and have fun—just like most kids throughout history. And kids still need to be engaged and spend time on task to learn. What is new are the specific technologies that kids find engaging, along with the tools that teachers may use to facilitate learning. *Teach Math with the Wii* equips educators with the skills and knowledge necessary to engage kids both physically and mentally, and to use technology as a tool to make learning both fun and effective.

I certainly wish my math teachers had such resources when I was a kid!

—Atsusi "2c" Hirumi

Atsusi "2c" Hirumi is an Associate Professor of Instructional Technology at the University of Central Florida. His books include Playing Games in School *(ISTE, 2010) and the* Grounded Designs for Online and Hybrid Learning *series (ISTE, 2013).*

PART I

Wii
GET INTO IT

By the end of 2012, over 99 million Nintendo Wii consoles and over 3 million Wii U's had been sold worldwide.

www.nintendo.co.jp/ir/library/historical_data/pdf/ consolidated_sales_e1212.pdf

Engaging Students
through
Gaming Technology

Welcome! We are ecstatic that this book has found its way to you. By now the juxtaposition of classroom instruction and using the Nintendo Wii may be floating around in your mind as it has in ours for some time. We look forward to exploring how to form a functional relationship between the two in the chapters to come.

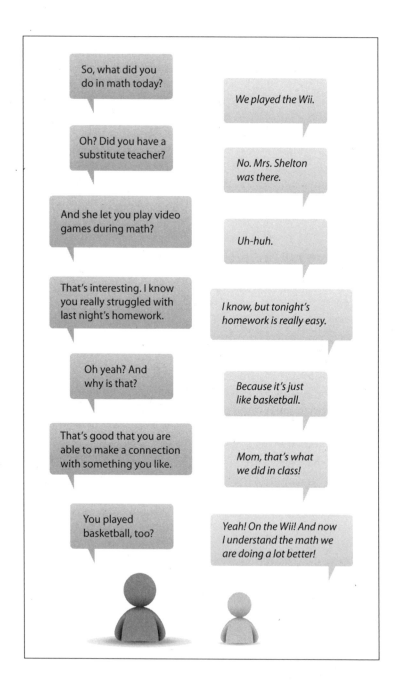

Before we get started, let us voice a few basic assumptions.

First, in selecting this book we assume that you are familiar with the Nintendo Wii video game console, though you need not have much or even any experience using the Wii in order to make good use of this content. Whether you are an expert gamer or a novice, our objective is to help support your use of the Wii as an educational tool for your students.

We also assume that you are familiar with the idea of using gaming technology to support instruction in the K–12 classroom. Perhaps your school already has several different video game consoles used in varying capacities throughout the building. Maybe your colleagues have been buzzing about adopting video games for classroom use and you're interested in learning more. We intend this book to be a relevant resource no matter where you are in the process, from deciding whether gaming technology is right for you, to acquiring Wii video game consoles for your school, to incorporating the Wii in math lessons as an invaluable instructional tool for engaging your learners.

Additionally, because you are considering this content, we presume that you demonstrate a willingness to reevaluate what instruction looks like in your math class. Bringing video games into the classroom will raise eyebrows and questions with students, colleagues, and parents. While you have their attention, why not impress them by flaunting exemplary standards-based instruction that allows learners to make real-life connections to their world through gaming technology? Undoubtedly, the Wii has strong entertainment value, but we recognize it has tremendous strength as an educational tool as well.

Changing Our Collective Outlook

"It's okay if math isn't your best subject. I was never any good at it either...."

A parent intends to comfort her child. Perhaps you have heard something like this before. A student struggles to the point of frustration in mathematics, but is not handed the tools to achieve academic success. Rather, failure is chalked up to a perceived genetic predisposition and a defeated attitude becomes the convenient coping mechanism. Parents aren't the only guilty party in this case. Many teachers have been known to make similar remarks. How we follow up these statements is what shapes the learner and her disposition, isn't it?

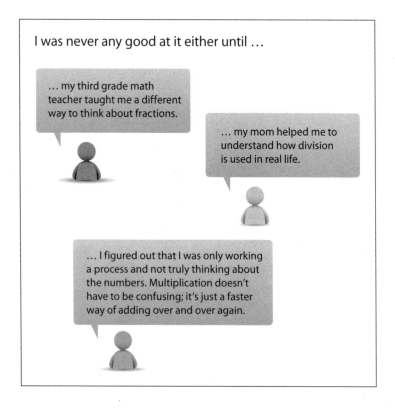

Our students have come to these sorts of realizations when given opportunities to explore math concepts using the Wii. Most of our students have experience playing the Wii at home, so we have automatic buy-in from the moment the students walk into the classroom and set eyes on the console. They have logged countless hours with their own consoles, setting new high scores, competing with friends, experiencing new worlds. What we offer as educators, however, is different. We approach the console as an instructional tool, identifying its potential to support our students in content areas where they are often struggling the most.

The key here is identifying instructional practices that reflect and honor the students' interests.

There are plenty of kids who struggle with mathematics, but good teachers recognize that dozens of factors may be at work. Supporting the student at home with homework is often a challenge for the parents. At school, there may be a mismatch between the instructional delivery and the student's learning style. Weaknesses in prerequisite skills on the learning trajectory may exist, making the student less successful with new concepts because of weaknesses in foundational concepts. The content may not strike the student as relevant, making new concepts more difficult to grasp. Instructional pacing may not be in sync with the student's learning pace. All of these obstacles can deter or delay a student's success in mathematics. Furthermore, the longer such hurdles remain in place, the less likely the student is to have positive encounters with mathematics.

Indisputably, a trend exists in all content areas to blame the failure to grasp concepts on the perception that the subject "just isn't my thing," "was never something I was good at," "is something I'll never get," or "my mom (or dad) was never good at it so I will never be good at it." However, research suggests that there is no "math gene" (www.maa.org/devlin/devlin_12_07.html). Consequently, these excuses hold absolutely no ground and are unacceptable. We must embrace the challenge of the child who struggles to see the value in mathematics by changing the way our mathematics instruction looks, feels, and sounds.

A Need for Change

We hold the assumption that you are an outstanding educator and you care about the success of your students. If you weren't, you likely would not have even bothered to browse a book about instruction. You also recognize that our world is changing and the way educators deliver instruction is evolving out of necessity to meet the needs of our students in this digital age.

We, as teachers, are charged with an incredible task: we are preparing our students to compete and succeed in a future world that we know little about because it does not yet exist. In it, our students will interface with technologies that have not yet been invented and compete for jobs that have not yet been created. Our world is growing and developing rapidly, and it is imperative that our classrooms and instructional practices reflect those of the global society.

Many doubtful people argue that one offender detracting from our students' academic success is the amount of time they spend in front of screens—many of us refer to it as "screen time." Televisions, smart phones, websites, tablets, handheld devices, and home consoles provide a constant stream of often unfiltered information and unending stimulation. How are we, as educators, supposed to compete with that? The answer is that we don't. We adapt. We bring the screens into the classroom, identifying the instructional value and application of these tools while recognizing the insatiable appetite our students have for using them.

It's exhilarating, actually, to introduce our students to another way of regarding the technology, because they do not expect it. No matter what fabulous technology tools already exist in your school, you still witness a few stunned faces when students realize that they will play the Wii in math today. Some tend to hold an "out there/ in here" idea of technology tools and they certainly are not afraid to express shock when they walk into your classroom and process that, yes, that is a Wii game image being projected larger than any TV they've ever seen and, yes, that is their teacher holding the Wii remote with what appears to be confidence, poise, and a glint of a challenge in her eyes.

The surprise wears off, but the effect is lasting.

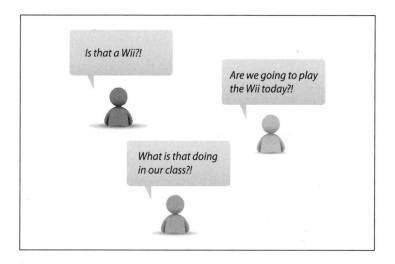

Another Piece of the Puzzle

We do not use the Wii for every single math lesson, nor do we imply in this book that we think you should. With that said, we have found the Wii to be an outstanding tool for helping students master math concepts with which they may otherwise struggle. Using this tool, like any math website, folder game, center activity, or read-aloud, is just a piece of the puzzle in supporting our learners. The Wii motivates our learners, helps establish a real-world connection to math concepts, and is familiar to a significant portion of our school population. That is why we believe it to be so powerful.

What sets the Wii apart from other tools of mathematics we employ is that students may actually have a Wii sitting in their family rooms or bedrooms, unlike Unifix cubes or other manipulatives. Based on the experience you share in class with your students, that Wii may now take on new meaning to a child who previously saw the console only for its entertainment value. Better yet, that child may see other mathematical connections in the games he or she is playing; connections that can be shared with classmates and may be the key to unlocking understanding within a given math concept for others.

As with learning any new topic or idea, there are cracks over which students stumble. In mathematics, these cracks might start out small but, over time, can manifest as significant achievement gaps. A recent study showed that approximately one-third of students entering two- and four-year colleges need to take a remedial mathematics or English course. That course will have an economic impact on the student, yet yield no college credit. Exemplary teachers like you are working to turn this statistic around by engaging students in the Standards for Mathematical Practice through many experiences, including the technologies students know and love.

One of the qualities we like most about using the Wii in math instruction is that it allows us to challenge students of a variety of skill levels through a single activity. We've intentionally written our Wii Math lessons with this in mind, and we hope you'll enjoy teaching these lessons as much as your students will enjoy participating in them.

Game On!

Well, this is it. Are you getting excited? Are your mental gears turning, picturing what this might look like in your classroom? Are you already anticipating your students' reactions and thinking that this might be the key to sparking their interest and unlocking their potential?

Make sure your batteries are fully charged and your screen is in focus. We have only hit the tip of the iceberg. On our journey, we will look at gaming technology from the eyes of a mathematics teacher, ways to obtain a Wii for your classroom or school at little or no cost to you, suggestions for promoting the Wii as an instructional tool to your school community, and, of course, a plethora of ready-to-teach lesson sparks aligned with Common Core State Standards for Mathematics.

Figure 1.1 Students attend to their classmate's turn at the Wii during a lesson.

Figure 1.2 As one student takes her turn, other students record the data.

So hit the power button, fasten your wrist strap, and make sure you've got plenty of room to move.

Game on!

Figure 1.3 Batter up! Each student is chosen randomly for his turn.

Think Like a Gamer, Think Like a Math Teacher

Picture this: The bell rings. The hallway teems with students packing up binders, stuffing homework into folders, shaking pencil cases, and chatting with friends. A line forms to enter the math classroom. As the students walk toward their desks, first one and then several of them notice a peculiar technology tool set up in the middle of the room. Conversation ensues....

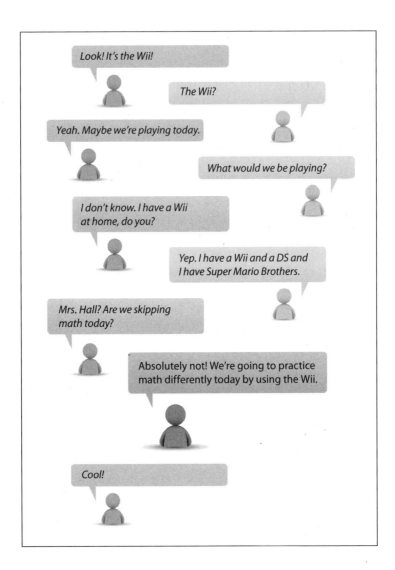

Math As We Knew It

Math classrooms have evolved over the past decades. So much so, in fact, that delivery of instruction now reflects student discovery, attainment, and mastery of concepts through the use of hands-on manipulatives, real-life application, and authentic exploration of new ideas. Learning is in the hands of our students, and teachers are charged with providing students with the necessary tools and learning environment to thrive. Communication and collaboration are now essential to our success.

It is critical for educators to be fluent in the language of their students, including their interests and those objects and experiences that motivate them most.

A Few Words from Matthew

I was introduced to the Nintendo Entertainment System (NES) at a friend's house when I was in second grade. I had grown up playing Atari games such as Frogger, Pac Man, and Pitfall, but it wasn't until playing the NES that I realized video games could be such a motivating tool for connecting with others, competing for high scores, and expressing creativity. I can still remember pretending to be Mario, the famed super plumber, as I raced around the playground with my friends, battling Koopa and his evil minions in order to save the princess.

I was a nerdy kid and I wear those experiences like badges of honor. I loved being in elementary school, but soon learned the hard truth that video games were for home and the playground. *Not* for school.

When you're at school, *you're there to learn.*

After 25 years (and a handful of video game consoles), I now work as a teacher librarian at an elementary school. One of the very first connections I made with students outside of sharing a passion for books was a mutual passion for video games. I strive, as I'm sure you do, to make personal connections with students throughout my instruction. I feel that the best way to reach the students is by connecting to their interests, and the best way to connect to their interests is to get to know them. My students love to excel and to participate in activities where they can succeed, even if it means making mistakes along the way. They are willing to try new things, and it's because of this willingness that Wii Math has taken off in our school.

Seeing the Math in the System

The Nintendo Wii is not inherently a math tool, but it holds up as a powerful motivator in the classroom and, in the hands of an educator, can exceed its role as an entertainment device to prove an effective instructional tool in the mathematics classroom.

The most rewarding part of designing the lessons included in this book has been finding the math in such an unlikely source. Although the games were designed for entertainment, many connections can be made between what is happening in the game and what is being studied in the math classroom, much as in any real-life application. When we approach the Wii for its implications in the classroom, we consider the standards students are working toward mastering. We then evaluate which game could support these skills, whether by using the game as a means to collect data for math computation or by observing the math naturally taking place when a person participates in the activity.

For example, parents shopping at the grocery store with young children will often draw deliberate connections to math by asking, "How many more things on our grocery list do we still need to find?" or "How many apples are in this bag?" Using bowling through the Wii Sports game, a teacher could just as easily ask students, "How many more pins did Emoni knock down than Tristan?" or "How many more pins would Tiana need in order to reach a score of 100?"

By seeing the math in these games, we facilitate our students' thinking about the Wii as a technology tool and challenge them to make meaningful connections to mathematics.

Meg Shares Some Thoughts

Because I think like a math teacher (hey, it's what I do), it was impossible for me to ignore the magnitude of the impact the Wii could have on budding mathematicians. As I began to explore the games with my children at home and at school, I found the mathematics embedded within the games to be obvious and begging for conversation. Each time I played a game, I developed questions that might prompt discourse or debate within a mathematics classroom. My greatest indicator of the power of this technology, however, was the level of engagement I witnessed each time I taught or co-taught a lesson using the device. To see the faces of each and every child in the class light up with joy when they realize that we are going to use the Wii during class is a highly motivating experience. Their celebrations of other classmates' successes were touching and sweet. The mathematics seemed to jump off the screen and be accessible to more students. Students who had never even used a Wii before were driven to participate and generate their own data. Others in the class looked on, attaching meaning to the numbers and recording the data in a table or some other organizer. To a math teacher, or any kind of teacher, this is all very exciting. Even more rewarding is the realization that each student is engaged in the mathematics, the discourse, and supporting their classmates as they "play" with mathematics.

Just as using children's literature can help students make connections to mathematical concepts and real-world contexts, the Wii games lend themselves to making similar connections. Wii games provide opportunities for students to solve problems that emerge from the data they generate. The lessons within this book demonstrate how to use a rich mathematical gaming experience to make connections to other mathematical ideas. Using this high-interest device in mathematics instruction helps students recognize how ideas in different areas of math, other subjects, or their own interests are related. We are all aware that it is important to have the opportunity to experience mathematics in context. Students should connect mathematical concepts to their daily lives, as well as to situations from other areas. Upon first using the Wii, I determined that students could recognize the value of mathematics in examining issues that are of importance to them and their social interests.

Students should be asked to communicate about the mathematics they are studying, to justify their reasoning with classmates, and to formulate questions about something that is puzzling or not immediately obvious. In doing so, they gain insights into their own thinking and the thinking of others. Communication becomes increasingly natural as students reflect on their learning and organize and consolidate their thinking about the mathematics they encounter within the games. When the vehicle for dialogue interests them, as the Wii does, students are further encouraged to express themselves coherently, clearly, and precisely using appropriate mathematical vocabulary.

As you progress through the grades, student argument and dialogue will more closely follow established classroom conventions, and students will become more aware of and responsive to the thinking of their peers. This will not, of course, happen without your skilled facilitation. Many of the lessons allow for collaborative work and problem solving. By working on problems with each other, students will have opportunities to see other perspectives and possible solutions. Your students can learn to understand and evaluate the thinking of others and expand upon those ideas through exposure to their peers' ideas. Students often benefit from engaging in conversations with other students who may choose to solve the problems in the lessons using a visual representation or some other approach. Experiences such as these increase student capacity to weigh the strengths and limitations of different approaches to the problems, causing them to think critically about mathematics. Opportunities to write about mathematics are also intentionally provided across the grades within our included lessons.

Figure 2.1 Meg recording data in the public space and facilitating discussions.

PART II

Wii-INTEGRATED
MATH LESSON SPARKS
AND COMMON CORE SUCCESS

By the beginning of 2012, Nintendo Wii's top-selling games included Wii Sports, Wii Sports Resort, and Wii Fit Plus with 79 million units, 29 million units, and 20 million units, respectively.

www.nintendo.co.jp/ir/pdf/2012/120127e.pdf#page=7

Wii Learning
and the
Common Core State Standards for Mathematics

This is an exciting time for mathematics instruction. The Common Core State Standards for Mathematics (CCSSM) provide a common framework for schools across the nation to share best practices so students will benefit. With students, parents, and teachers working together toward shared goals, students will make progress each year and graduate prepared to be successful—building a strong future for themselves and the world in which we live.

Leveling the Playing Field

Up to this point, almost every state has had its own set of mathematics standards, each different in some manner. When students move between states, the differences between the curricula become obvious. If a student moves to a state that has more rigorous standards, she may struggle to work on grade level in the new state. This can be very confusing and disappointing to both students and parents.

The CCSSM define what students should understand and be able to do in their study of mathematics. In order to evaluate student understanding of mathematics, we ask teachers to assess what students understand. Thus the question, "What does mathematical understanding look like?" comes to the forefront of educators' minds. Students need to justify why a particular mathematical statement is true or determine from where a mathematical rule or procedure might come. While some students may be able to solve a problem procedurally, many struggle with a response if asked why procedures work. Students who can explain a procedure understand the mathematics in greater depth, and may have a better opportunity to succeed at a related but less-familiar task. Mathematical understanding and procedural skill are both important, and each can be assessed as students engage in lesson sparks.

The eight Standards for Mathematical Practice "describe varieties of expertise that mathematics educators at all levels should seek to develop in their students" (www.corestandards.org/Math/Practice). The practices are how we engage in the mathematics at hand.

Standards for Mathematical Practice

1. Make sense of problems and persevere in solving them.

2. Reason abstractly and quantitatively.

3. Construct viable arguments and critique the reasoning of others.

4. Model with mathematics.

5. Use appropriate tools strategically.

6. Attend to precision.

7. Look for and make use of structure.

8. Look for and express regularity in repeated reasoning.

These Standards for Mathematical Practice apply to all students from Kindergarten through Grade 12. Students are expected to develop and apply these practices in mathematics classrooms and beyond, and that is where the teacher's questioning skills will be essential. Consider how the CCSSM may look in your classroom, remembering that students in all grades are charged with engaging with mathematics through these eight standards. Similarly, all teachers will hone their facilitator skills, so their students will actively engage in the practices. In each of the lessons outlined in the following chapters, you will find suggested questions teachers can pose to ensure that students will apply the Standards for Mathematical Practice.

For example, consider the following Measurement and Data (MD) Grade 2 standard, 2.MD.5, that asks students to solve addition and subtraction word problems involving lengths within 100:

> Use addition and subtraction within 100 to solve word prob-
> lems involving lengths that are given in the same units, e.g.,
> by using drawings (such as drawings of rulers) and equations
> with a symbol for the unknown number to represent the
> problem. (www.corestandards.org/Math/Content/2/MD/B/5)

Table 3.1 illustrates how the eight Standards for Mathematical Practice could be integrated while students are playing Tightrope Walk, an activity on Wii Fit Plus in which players demonstrate balance by walking on a tightrope suspended between two build-ings. In column two, we examine how Standard 2.MD.5 might look in a classroom in which students are engaged in the Standards for Mathematical Practice.

TABLE 3.1 Evidence of the Eight Practices within a Wii Math Lesson

CC Standard for Mathematical Practice	Evidence of the practice using lengths in Wii Tightrope Walk (Lesson Spark 2.6, Standard 2.MD.5)
1. Make sense and persevere in solving problems	Students make sense of the context and find a way to explore the problem using objects or drawings.
2. Reason abstractly and quantitatively	Students can decontextualize the problem and match quantities to the total distance. Further, students can contextualize the quantities and explain what each quantity represents.
3. Construct viable arguments and critique the reasoning of others	Students make a clear argument to defend their strategy. Students accurately evaluate their classmates' strategies.
4. Model with mathematics	Students create an equation to match their strategy and work. In our extension example, this could be $46 + \_\_ = 94$ or $94 - 46 = \_\_$.
5. Use appropriate tools strategically	Students successfully use objects (e.g., base-ten blocks) or pictures to support their work.
6. Attend to precision	Students communicate their process using visual models and written explanations. Their answers are accurate and clear.
7. Look for and make use of structure	Students apply structure of our base-ten number system to support their work. In this example, students may start at 46 and recognize that if they skip count by tens, they eventually get to 96 and then can count back by ones to reach 94.
8. Look for and express regularity in repeated reasoning	While solving future problems, students use known information to help them. For example, a student may reason, "I know that when I have a missing addend, I can start with my first number and count up. So I am going to start at 46 and then count up until I get to 94."

We do not presume that all of the eight Standards for Mathematical Practice will be evident in every lesson spark included in this book. However, we make a concerted effort to incorporate opportunities for as many standards as possible in each lesson spark. Before teaching the lessons, we highly recommend that teachers take time to consider how these eight Standards for Mathematical Practice will be implemented consistently in their classroom. In Appendix A, you will find a table illustrating the correlation of the Wii lesson sparks and Common Core State Standards for Mathematics.

In our experience, teachers are vested in understanding what their students are expected to do. Bear in mind that the CCSSM outline the rigor necessary for career and college readiness. Reaching each standard requires a depth of understanding and proficiency that will take time to develop. Educators are looking forward to having more time to delve into concepts and build greater student capacity for applying knowledge to a variety of problem scenarios. Because the CCSSM outline how concepts evolve and build upon each other, expectations for student learning are clear and learning trajectories can be traced through the grades. Table 3.1 illustrates merely one example of how the Standards for Mathematical Practice might be evident within a lesson.

Obviously, the widespread adoption of the CCSSM indicates that this is a time of change for mathematics instruction in the United States. Knowing the huge impact this change will have, we thought it would be useful to provide opportunities for engaging the eight Standards of Mathematical Practice within our lessons. This idea naturally evolved into writing the lessons to show how the CCSSM might look in a classroom by identifying the standards each lesson would meet. Thus, the lessons included in this book take into consideration both the CCSSM and the eight Standards for Mathematical Practice. As the teacher, you will want to reflect on the specific actions you will take to involve students in the Standards for Mathematical Practice before you teach the lessons.

Universal Design for Learning

In addition to the reform marked by the CCSSM, the United States' education system has seen a movement toward Universal Design for Learning (UDL). UDL is a framework for curriculum design that fosters access to learning for all types of learners. UDL recognizes that every learner is unique and processes information differently. We have designed our lessons with this framework in mind. UDL is based on research about how the brain learns and incorporates the new digital media. In addition, UDL helps to identify and eliminate barriers from teaching methods and curriculum materials, allowing each student to engage in learning and progress. UDL also addresses each learner's unique needs, background, and interests by supporting individualized methods, materials, and assessments.

Kinesthetic Learning and UDL

One instructional approach central to UDL is the practice of providing multiple means through which students can explore concepts and work toward skill mastery. Teachers exercise this practice when they incorporate movement into their instruction. Movement is central to many games for the Wii, especially those used in the lessons within this book.

Many physical education classes throughout the U.S. have been quick to adopt the Nintendo Wii and Wii Fit balance board for their programs, employing video games as a tool to encourage students to adopt more active lifestyles. In fact, many experts believe that good physical fitness habits may facilitate learning. While video games are often pinned as contributors to the growing childhood obesity rates, these teachers aim to harness a central interest of their students in order to motivate them to be more active in PE class. Students who had not considered themselves athletic and were often disengaged in class found a platform where they could outperform even their most athletic peers, playing games such as Dance Dance Revolution. Given the link between fitness and learning, many educators believe that using kinesthetic methods in academic lessons will encourage students to get moving and, ultimately, perform better academically.

Some educators advocate the use of kinesthetic methods in academic lessons, believing that some students have a kinesthetic learning style, and that these students are better learners when material is presented in a kinesthetic mode. A similar situation is apparent in many math classrooms: students who struggle with specific concepts are often not engaged and, therefore, are not learning. For some students, meaningful movement allows them to interact differently with concepts and form lasting understandings. This is one example of why we believe that the Wii is an effective tool to support math instruction. When students are active in the classroom, whether by taking a turn playing the preselected Wii game or at their seats, practicing the correct form for the game by arching an arm in an imaginary three-point shot or swinging an invisible bat to time the perfect hit, they are activating prior knowledge, making connections to these movements, and exploring math concepts. This provides them with a platform to connect the movement of the sport to the math within that same sport.

Kinesthetic Learning and the Wii

Today, teachers are expected to engage all of their students, allow them to learn with all their senses, and move purposefully around the classroom as part of the learning process. Many educators understand this and frequently employ kinesthetic methods in their lessons. By incorporating the Wii into our lessons, we found a simple and natural way to engage students and appeal to the kinesthetic mode of learning.

There are a number of benefits to these movements, the first and foremost being that the students are physically active, stimulating blood circulation and increasing alertness, awareness, and brain activity. The students are also improving muscle memory for those movements required in each sport. Our lesson sparks suggest that teachers accommodate the varying needs of their students by using multisensory instruction to improve academic performance.

Because our students all learn differently and become engaged through a wide variety of stimuli, we have developed what we feel is a robust collection of lesson sparks designed to engage and motivate students while allowing them to explore the identified standards through multiple learning devices. Our lessons provide options for eliminating barriers and engaging students in mathematics learning.

Online UDL Resources

You can learn more about UDL and access a wealth of resources through the following websites:

- The National Center on Universal Design for Learning (www.udlcenter.org)
- Center for Applied Special Technology (www.cast.org)

Take Time to Reflect

As you incorporate the lessons in this book into your teaching, we encourage you to take time to reflect on your experiences. We often found our classes to be more lively, our students to be more engaged in the lesson, and the variety of students contributing to the discussion to be more diverse and robust.

Consider the following questions while you reflect on a specific math lesson in which you incorporated the Wii:

- What was the level of engagement in your classroom during this lesson?

- What did you observe about the student learning taking place during the lesson?

- How did you observe your students making sense and persevering in solving problems during the lesson?

- What viable arguments did your students construct and how did they critique the reasoning of others?

- How did your students model with mathematics?

- What tools did your students use appropriately and strategically?

- What evidence did you see of your students attending to precision?

- How did your students look for and make use of structure?

- When did your students look for and express regularity in repeated reasoning?

You will undoubtedly be able to recognize whether the lesson was a success by the students' correct use of the vocabulary associated with the math concept being reinforced and their ability to make a connection between that concept and the real-world scenario simulated in the game. You will want to guide the discussion and ensure accuracy with mathematics vocabulary through modeling. Pay close attention not only to those students who are playing the Wii, but also to the students who are watching from their desks, recording data, working on computations, and otherwise engaging in the lesson. Facilitate the dialogue by strategically posing open-ended questions. As in any other math lesson, you are watching for the students' ability to demonstrate mastery of the skill. This will, of course, develop over time. It's possible, however, to observe the rate at which your students are able to connect the gaming going on with the lesson's content focus.

In making these observations ourselves, we have noticed that a greater number of students appear to make meaningful connections with the concepts being taught or reinforced early on in the lesson. Exploring the concept through play allows students to make authentic connections to the content in ways that they may not have otherwise experienced. We have found proof of student success in their level of interest in the lesson and subsequent discussion. By using the Wii, we appeal to students' interest in technology and capture their natural curiosity about mathematics, increasing their willingness to take a risk and participate in the classroom dialogue while engaged in the Standards for Mathematical Practice.

Conclusion

Following this chapter you will find a bank of math lesson sparks that are aligned with the CCSSM for Kindergarten through Grade 7 (ages 5–13). These lesson sparks can be used to teach, reinforce, or review mathematical concepts with students. Each lesson spark incorporates the Wii in a unique way. As both of us have observed, embracing this familiar technology tool can have a profound effect on motivating students and providing those real-world experiences necessary to make meaningful connections with new concepts.

Wii Sports, Wii Sports Resort, and Wii Fit Plus
in the Math Class

This chapter contains six lesson sparks for each grade level K–7, making a total of 48 sparks. The lesson sparks are coded K.1–K.6, 1.1–1.6, and 2.1–2.6 for primary grades (ages 5–8); 3.1–3.6, 4.1–4.6, and 5.1–5.6 for intermediate grades (ages 8–11); and 6.1–6.6 and 7.1–7.6 for grades 6 and 7 (ages 11–13 and gifted and talented students ages 9 and up).

Which Wii Game?

The lesson sparks for K.1–5.6 use Wii Sports, Wii Sports Resort, and Wii Fit Plus. As shown in Table 4.1, the lesson sparks suggested for Grades 6 and 7 (ages 11–13 or higher-performing younger students) call for Wii Sports Resort and Wii Fit Plus only.

TABLE 4.1 Which Wii Game You'll Need by Grade

Game	Primary grades			Intermediate grades			Grades 6–7	
	K	1	2	3	4	5	6	7
Wii Sports	✔	✔	✔	✔	✔	✔		
Wii Sports Resort	✔	✔	✔	✔	✔	✔	✔	✔
Wii Fit Plus	✔	✔	✔	✔	✔	✔	✔	✔

What Gear?

Table 4.2 shows the basic gear you will need for the lesson sparks. When playing multiplayer games, you will need additional controllers. Note that although it is possible to play Wii Sports and Wii Fit Plus with a standard Wii controller, the MotionPlus controller is required to play Wii Sports Resort. You will need at least two MotionPlus controllers to support multiplayer games. Chapter 5 includes additional details on the Wii equipment you will need and various ways to procure it.

TABLE 4.2 What Each Wii Will Need

Gear needed	Wii Sports	Wii Sports Resort	Wii Fit Plus
Nintendo Wii console	✔	✔	✔
Wii Sports game disc	✔		
Wii Sports Resort game disc		✔	
Wii Fit Plus game disc			✔
Wii Fit balance board			✔
Nintendo nunchuk controllers	✔	✔	✔
Wii MotionPlus controllers		✔	✔

Wii U

On November 28, 2012, Nintendo launched its newest console: Wii U. The console was released during the course of our writing this book and we felt it best to focus primarily on the Wii and its games wherein our primary experience is based. However, there are several exciting implications of which we feel you should be made aware. The Wii U is backwards compatible, meaning standard Wii games can be played on the new console. What is better is that the controllers and additional hardware, such as the nunchuks and Wii Fit balance board, are also compatible with the Wii U. Because data (saved games and downloaded content) can easily be transferred to the Wii U from the Wii, some Wii U owners may now be looking to sell or re-home their Wii consoles. Additionally, the cost of new Wii consoles is now on the decline thanks to the new console release. Canadian citizens can purchase the Wii Mini, a compact Wii console, at a reduced price with all of the great qualities of the Wii minus the ability to connect to the Internet.

Lesson Sparks

The 48 lesson sparks are divided into three sections: Primary Grades, Intermediate Grades, and Grades 6 and 7.

Lesson Sparks for Primary Grades (K–2, Ages 5–8)

Students in primary grades are still developing hand-eye coordination and often struggle with accuracy when playing these Wii games. When we work with such students, we often set aside time to model how to play the game, including having the whole class practice the movements used within the game itself. During the activity, some students may need the kind of guidance one would expect a golf instructor to offer a person learning to golf for the first time. That is to say, we often find ourselves shadowing the students and assisting them in moving the correct way for the first several turns. As soon as we get the sense that the student is picking up the skill, we back away and let them take over.

Considering this, the following lesson sparks incorporate games students can be successful playing with little to no prior experience. However, we strongly recommend that you, the educator, familiarize yourself with each game before you play it with students. As you do, consider what game aspects may be challenging for them—such as timing, coordination, and the concept of how to play the game successfully—so that you can anticipate any challenges that may arise during the lesson.

You'll most likely be surprised at how quickly the students pick things up, especially when it comes to playing video games. Most of the actions with the remote incorporated in each game are intuitive to the sport itself. This quality assures that even the most amateur of players can actually do very well from the start.

TABLE 4.3 Wii Games for Primary Grade Sparks K.1–2.6

Grade	Wii Sports	Wii Sports Resort	Wii Fit Plus
K	K.1, K.2	K.3, K.4	K.5, K.6
1	1.1, 1.2	1.3, 1.4	1.5, 1.6
2	2.1, 2.2	2.3, 2.4	2.5, 2.6

Kindergarten Lesson Sparks (Ages 5–6)

K.1
Wii Bowl and Make 10

Game Used
Wii Sports Bowling

Common Core Math Standard
(K.OA.4). For any number from 1 to 9, find the number that makes 10 when added to the given number, e.g., by using objects or drawings, and record the answer with a drawing or equation.

Description of Lesson/Activities
Students take turns generating scores by bowling a frame (two throws). Rather than using the cumulative score for the frame, you may wish to allow students to choose which score (the number of pins knocked over by the first or second ball) they want to use. For example, if a student missed all of the pins on the first ball, he or she would have a 0. But if on his second ball in the frame he knocked over 4 pins, he could choose which number (0 or 4) he wanted to represent. As other students take their turns, have the spectators represent their score using counters and ten-frames, base-ten blocks, Rekenreks, or Digi-Blocks. Ask students to record the numeral in their math journal. As students record the information in their journals, ask them questions such as, "How far is that number from 10?" or "What is a number that is 1 (or 2) more (or less)?" or "Is that number even or odd? How do you know?" Once

all students have taken their turn, direct them to a partner and ask them to record all of the make-ten equations that they can.

K.2
Wii Compare Numbers

Game Used
Wii Sports Bowling (2 Players)

Common Core Math Standard
(K.CC.7) Compare two numbers between 1 and 10 presented as written numerals.

Description of Lesson/Activities

Two students at a time take turns generating scores by bowling a frame. Rather than using the cumulative score for the frame, you may wish to allow students to choose which score (the number of pins knocked over by the first or second ball) they want to use. For example, if a student missed all of the pins on the first ball, he or she would have a 0. But if on his second ball in the frame he knocked over 4 pins, he could choose which number (0 or 4) he wanted to represent. The teacher should record the numbers from both students on the board or in the public space. Have the spectators represent each player's score using counters and ten-frames (optional), base-ten blocks, Rekenreks, or Digi-Blocks. Ask students to also record each player's numeral in their math journal. As students record the information in their journals, ask them questions comparing two of the scores such as, "Which number is larger (or greater or more)?" and "Which number is smaller (or least or less)?" and "How do you know?" Once all students

> ### Common Core Codes
>
> Domain abbreviations such as *OA*, *CC*, *G*, and *NBT* are spelled out in Appendix A. *K.CC* stands for Grade K Counting and Cardinality, for example. And *1.OA* stands for Grade 1 Operations and Algebraic Thinking.

have taken a turn, direct them to a partner and ask them to find the difference in the values they each scored on their turns by lining up their counters and comparing. Depending on the need for student extension, you may also ask partners to record the equations used to determine the difference.

K.3
Wii Speed Slice Still Life

Game Used
Wii Sports Resort Swordplay: Speed Slice

Common Core Math Standard
(K.G.1) Describe objects in the environment using names of shapes, and describe the relative positions of these objects using terms such as *above, below, beside, in front of, behind,* and *next to.*

Description of Lesson/Activities
Introduce the lesson by having students demonstrate the following positions relative to a classroom object such as a desk or chair: *above, below, beside, in front of, behind, on, far away from, around,* and *within.* Using two student volunteers, create a "still life" drawing of objects sliced throughout a game of Speed Slice. Pausing after each round, draw the first object sliced in the middle of your "canvas" (chalkboard, marker board, paper, etc.). Draw an outline of each subsequent object using a different relative position to the original object. For example, if the first object sliced was a pencil, you might draw the next object *beside* the pencil or *under* the pencil. After 5–7 rounds of demonstration, direct students to their seats and distribute paper and drawing utensils. Have two new students participate in the Speed Slice game while the remaining students

Preview Games First

Is slicing a virtual piece of fruit into pieces with a virtual sword (Spark K.3) an act of violence? Preview all games with your students' and their parents' sensibilities in mind.

create still-life drawings based on what is sliced. Select a number between 3 and 10 to determine how many objects to draw, then provide students with a relative position in which they will draw their object after each round. You may wish to draw along with the students in order to help model instruction. After students have completed drawing the objects sliced in the selected number of rounds, they may complete their still-life drawings by coloring them.

K.4
Wii Do Airborne Math

Game Used
Wii Sports Resort Air Sports: Skydiving

Common Core Math Standard
(K.OA.3) Decompose numbers less than or equal to 10 into pairs in more than one way, e.g., by using objects or drawings, and record each decomposition by a drawing or equation (e.g., 5 = 2 + 3 and 5 = 4 + 1).

Description of Lesson/Activities
Introduce the lesson by showing students a collection of dolls or figures (up to 10). Tell them a story about how you went skydiving over the weekend and how you grabbed hands with jump partners while you were in the air. Show a set number of dolls or figures and tell students you grabbed hands with that many people throughout your jump. Ask students what two numbers add together for a sum equivalent to your number (e.g., 7 = 3 + 4), then tell students that when you jumped you actually grabbed hands with people matching their equation (e.g., "First I grabbed hands with 3 people, then we let go and I grabbed hands with 4 people"). Ask, "What other numbers add together to get my sum?" Demonstrate the Skydiving game by selecting a student volunteer and drawing attention to the total number of connected people throughout the game (those whose picture the photographer snaps). Pause the game after each picture and ask students, "What two numbers add together to equal the total number of people connected at the time of the

photo?" Have students represent this equation by using manipulatives such as colored chips or marbles. You may switch student participants after each pause of the game, or after several turns at connecting with other jumpers. For larger numbers, combine the scores from consecutive pictures, then ask students to decompose the sum into two addends. Encourage students to represent each of the possible addend pairs for each score, prompting students with questions such as, "I see that (student name) showed 7 is the same as 5 + 2. Is 5 + 2 also the same as 2 + 5?" and "I've walked around the room and noticed that 2 + 5, 4 + 3, and 0 + 7 all equal 7. Are there any other number pairs that add to 7?" Repeat until all students have had an opportunity to participate.

K.5
Perfect 10

Game Used
Wii Fit Plus Training Plus: Perfect 10

Common Core Math Standard
(K.OA.3) Decompose numbers less than or equal to 10 into pairs in more than one way, e.g., by using objects or drawings, and record each decomposition by a drawing or equation (e.g., 5 = 2 + 3 and 5 = 4 + 1).

Description of Lesson/Activities
Students take turns rotating their hips to bop the addends that will make 10. As the student demonstrates fluency with this, the game will introduce the player's ability to use three addends and negative numbers (if it comes up, I just tell them they are subtracting or taking away). When other students take their turns, have the spectators represent their score using a ten-frame and counters or Rekenreks. You may ask students to record

One More Bunny

You may wish to accompany your K.5 lesson by reading aloud *One More Bunny: Adding from One to Ten* by Rick Walton.

their equations in their journals or on a piece of paper. If you notice a student hesitating or struggling, you might ask, "How far is that number from 10?" or "What strategy might you use to figure this one out?" or "Do you know a related fact that might help you?" Once all students have taken a turn, direct them to a partner and ask them to share which make-ten fact is hardest for them. Ask students to share their strategies for figuring out the other addends. If time allows, ask students to work with a new partner, repeating the previous direction.

K.6
Wii Do a Little Head-Butting

Game Used
Wii Fit Plus Balance Games: Soccer Heading

Common Core Math Standards
(K.CC.1) Count to 100 by ones and by tens.

(K.CC.2) Count forward beginning from a given number within the known sequence (instead of having to begin at 1).

Description of Lesson/Activities
With the class gathered together, hold a soccer ball in your hands. Ask the class to move their bodies so that, if the soccer ball were thrown, the ball would bounce off their foreheads. Practice by positioning the ball above your head, to the far right or left, and degrees in between, all the while asking students to adjust their position so that they can headbutt the ball. Ask students to predict how many balls they think they could headbutt in real life, then demonstrate how to headbutt soccer balls on Wii Fit Plus. Allow a student volunteer to play one round of Soccer and record the number of points he or she scored on the blackboard or in the public space. Distribute individual hundreds charts and/or draw the students' attention to an oversized class hundreds chart. Ask, "How many points total would the student have if he/she scored 5 more points?" Locate the student's score on the hundreds chart and count up five numbers

or write the proceeding five numbers on the blackboard beside the original number. Repeat until all students have had an opportunity to play, each time asking students to count up from the score to a given number of points. In time, challenge students to count up without the aid of the hundreds chart.

First Grade Lesson Sparks (Ages 6–7)

1.1
Word Problem Home-Run Derby

Game Used
Wii Sports Baseball (Training): Hitting Home Runs

Common Core Math Standard
(1.OA.1) Use addition and subtraction within 20 to solve word problems involving situations of adding to, taking from, putting together, taking apart, and comparing, with unknowns in all positions, e.g., by using objects, drawings, and equations with a symbol for the unknown number to represent the problem.

Description of Lesson/Activities
Record the names of participants and scores in the public area as each student takes a turn in Hitting Home Runs. After each student has had an opportunity to participate, use the student data to create word problems. Word problems can be created on the spot in front of the students and recorded in the public area for students to solve. You may also choose to create a template for word problems ahead of time, leaving out specific names of students and associated data for the problems. Have students complete the computation for each word problem in their math journal.

Sample word-problem templates:

- Student A hit 5 home runs. Student B hit 7 home runs. How many home runs did Student A and Student B hit altogether?

- Student A and Student B hit 12 home runs. Student C and Student D hit 8 home runs. How many more home runs did Student A and Student B hit?

- Student A hit 6 home runs. Student A and another student hit 11 home runs altogether. How many home runs did the other student hit?

1.2
Bowling Give or Take

Game Used
Wii Sports Bowling (Training): Power Throws

Common Core Math Standard
(1.NBT.5) Given a two-digit number, mentally find 10 more or 10 less than the number, without having to count; explain the reasoning used.

Description of Lesson/Activities
Introduce the lesson by showing students various collections of objects (such as a jar of buttons, a tub of pencils, a cup of crayons, etc.). Tell the students how many objects are in each container, then ask the class to determine how many there would be if 10 were added to or taken away from the container. Demonstrate with the students by adding 10 of the object to the container's total, counting aloud as you add each object. Likewise, demonstrate taking away 10 of the object. Allow a student volunteer to play one frame of Power Throws. Using manipulatives or a hundreds chart, have each student determine how many 10 more of the score would be. Repeat this process for the remainder of the game, allowing each student to participate in one frame of the game and having students determine how many 10 more or less of the score would be.

1.3
Wii Take Aim

Game Used
Wii Sports Resort Archery

Common Core Math Standard
(1.NBT.3) Compare two two-digit numbers based on meanings of the tens and ones digits, recording the results of comparisons with the symbols >, =, and <.

Description of Lesson/Activities
Review the standard with students by rolling two pairs of dice and recording the two-digit numbers in the public space. Represent the value of the ones and tens places using symbols, then compare the value of the ones place in each score. "Which number has a greater digit in the ones place? How do you know?" Compare the values of the tens place in each score. "Which number has a greater digit in the tens place? How do you know?" After comparing, ask students which of the two numbers is bigger. Compare the two numbers by writing >, <, or =. If needed, roll the pairs of dice again and compare the numbers. Try to compare two numbers with the same ones place or the same tens place. After practicing this comparison, model the archery game, demonstrating the objective of the game and modeling how the controls work. Select two student volunteers to participate in the archery game. Have each student complete one round of archery (four arrows) and record each score on the board or in the public space. Ask students to record each score side-by-side in their math journals. Call attention to the number in the tens place for each score. Ask, "Which of these scores has a higher number in the tens place?" and "What does this tell us about this score in comparison to the other score?" In the space between the digits, compare the two numbers by writing <, >, or =. After each student has completed the problem, ask a student volunteer to read aloud his or her math sentence (e.g., "24 is greater than 14"). Repeat this activity, comparing pairs of scores until each student in the class has participated.

1.4

Table Tennis Tens and Ones

Game Used
Wii Sports Resort Table Tennis: Table Tennis Return

Common Core Math Standards
(1.NBT.2) Understand that the two digits of a two-digit number represent amounts of tens and ones. Understand the following as special cases:

- (1.NBT.2a) 10 can be thought of as a bundle of ten ones—called a "ten."

- (1.NBT.2b) The numbers from 11 to 19 are composed of a ten and one, two, three, four, five, six, seven, eight, or nine ones.

- (1.NBT.2c) The numbers 10, 20, 30, 40, 50, 60, 70, 80, 90 refer to one, two, three, four, five, six, seven, eight, or nine tens (and 0 ones).

Description of Lesson/Activities
Introduce the activity by rolling two dice and recording the results as a two-digit number. Record the number on the board or in the public space. Represent the value of the ones digit by drawing a corresponding number of circles arranged in an array. Likewise, represent the value of the tens digit by drawing squares. As a class, read the two-digit number as well as the value of its digits (e.g., "26, or 2 tens and 6 ones"). Have a student volunteer demonstrate how to play Table Tennis Return. Record the score from the volunteer and represent the score in the public space using circles to represent the number of ones and squares to represent the number of tens. As each remaining student has the opportunity to participate in the game, have students record his or her score in their math journals while you record the score in the public space. Next, have students represent the ones and tens values through drawing the correct corresponding number of circles and squares. Ask, "Which of our scores today had the greatest number of ones? The greatest number of tens? What is the lowest score we recorded today? What is the highest score?"

1.5
Table Tilt Comparisons

Game Used
Wii Fit Plus Balance Games: Table Tilt

Common Core Math Standards
(1.NBT.2) Understand that the two digits of a two-digit number represent amounts of tens and ones. Understand the following as special cases:

- (1.NBT.2a) 10 can be thought of as a bundle of ten ones—called a "ten."

- (1.NBT.2b) The numbers from 11 to 19 are composed of a ten and one, two, three, four, five, six, seven, eight, or nine ones.

- (1.NBT.2c) The numbers 10, 20, 30, 40, 50, 60, 70, 80, 90 refer to one, two, three, four, five, six, seven, eight, or nine tens (and 0 ones).

(1.NBT.3) Compare two two-digit numbers based on meanings of the tens and ones digits, recording the results of comparisons with the symbols >, =, and <.

(1.NBT.5) Given a two-digit number, mentally find 10 more or 10 less than the number, without having to count; explain the reasoning used.

(1.NBT.6) Subtract multiples of 10 in the range 10–90 from multiples of 10 in the range 10–90 (positive or zero differences), using concrete models or drawings and strategies based on place value, properties of operations, and/or the relationship between addition and subtraction; relate the strategy to a written method and explain the reasoning used.

Description of Lesson/Activities
Students alternate playing the game to generate a two-digit number. Spectators will record the number and represent it using a tens and ones place-value mat and base-ten blocks or Digi-Blocks. Have students use the place-value recording sheet to record how many tens and ones are in each score. Ask students, "What is 10 more (or less) than your value?" and "How do you know?" Partner students and ask them to choose a value that they recorded and compare it with their partner's chosen value. Ask students to record some other subtraction equations they can think of that subtract a tens value from their value (example: 57 – 20 = 37). Allow them to

use base-ten blocks or Digi-Blocks to solve them as appropriate. Depending on the need for student extension, you may also offer a hundreds chart and ask, "How far is that value from 100 (or 90, or some other tens value)?"

1.6
Wii Compare Penguin Slide

Game Used
Wii Fit Plus Balance Games: Penguin Slide

Common Core Math Standards
(1.NBT.3) Compare two two-digit numbers based on meanings of the tens and ones digits, recording the results of comparisons with the symbols >, =, and <.

(1.NBT.4) Add within 100, including adding a two-digit number and a one-digit number, and adding a two-digit number and a multiple of 10, using concrete models or drawings and strategies based on place value, properties of operations, and/or the relationship between addition and subtraction; relate the strategy to a written method and explain the reasoning used. Understand that in adding two-digit numbers, one adds tens and tens, ones and ones; and sometimes it is necessary to compose a ten.

Description of Lesson/Activities
Students take turns generating scores by playing the game. Spectator students work in pairs. Each student will record the double-digit score of one of their classmates. Partners cannot record the same student's score. Have the spectators also represent the players' scores using base-ten blocks or Digi-Blocks (you may also wish to distribute hundreds charts for student reference). Ask students to record each player's numeral in their math journal with the appropriate symbol (>, <, or =) in between the two numbers. As students record the information in their journals, ask them questions such as, "Which number is greater?" and "Which number is least?" and "How do you know?" or "How far is your number from the next (or previous) ten?" As players take their turns, you might record in the public space their score with one of the symbols next

to it and inquire, "What number could I write here (referring to the blank) to make a true statement?" Once all students have taken their turn, direct them back to their partner and ask them to find the sum of their values.

Second Grade Lesson Sparks (Ages 7–8)

2.1
Target Practice Golf

Game Used
Wii Sports Golf (Training): Target Practice

Common Core Math Standards
(2.NBT.5) Fluently add and subtract within 100 using strategies based on place value, properties of operations, and/or the relationship between addition and subtraction.

(2.NBT.7) Add and subtract within 1000, using concrete models or drawings and strategies based on place value, properties of operations, and/or the relationship between addition and subtraction; relate the strategy to a written method. Understand that in adding or subtracting three-digit numbers, one adds or subtracts hundreds and hundreds, tens and tens, ones and ones; and sometimes it is necessary to compose or decompose tens or hundreds.

(2.MD.10) Draw a picture graph and a bar graph (with single-unit scale) to represent a data set with up to four categories. Solve simple put-together, take-apart, and compare problems using information presented in a bar graph.

Description of Lesson/Activities
Students take turns generating scores by hitting the ball at the target. As students generate scores, ask them to keep a running total for the game using a strategy. Ten turns make a game, so students will compare the final scores for two games, finding the difference and sum of the game scores. Ask students, "How far is your score from 100?" and "Is it closer to 0, 50, or 100?" As each student takes a turn, ask them to record their individual score on a sticky note. After each student has taken a turn, direct students

to place their sticky notes on a piece of chart paper with all of the same scores together in a category, thus creating a bar graph of the student data. Ask students, "What score was hit the most?" and "What can you tell me about the data?"

2.2
Batting Practice

Game Used
Wii Sports Baseball (Training): Batting Practice

Common Core Math Standard
(2.OA.1) Use addition and subtraction within 100 to solve one- and two-step word problems involving situations of adding to, taking from, putting together, taking apart, and comparing, with unknowns in all positions, e.g., by using drawings and equations with a symbol for the unknown number to represent the problem.

Description of Lesson/Activities

Begin the lesson by asking students to take out a pencil and open their math journals or take out a sheet of paper. Share with the students that you just scored an all-time personal best in Baseball Batting Practice: 16 points! Ask students the following:

- How many more points would I need to hit a perfect score of 30 hits?

- How many more points is this score compared to my all-time low of 3 points?

Students may calculate the answers mentally or on paper, using any strategy they choose. After discussing the answer, allow students the opportunity to take turns generating scores by hitting the ball. Remind students to record their own scores in their journal or on paper. (Note: The maximum score possible in this game is 30 hits.) Once each student or a small group of students has had the opportunity to participate, ask students to use their data in order to answer the following problems set in context:

- Tynese scored a total of 29 hits during her batting practice. You scored _____ hits. How many more hits did she score?

- Hadley scored 19 points on her first try at bat. You scored _____ hits. What is the total of your scores combined?

- You scored _____ points. How many hits did Skyler score if your combined total was 51 hits?

- Caleb scored 27 points. You scored _____ points. How many more points would it take to reach a total of 100 points?

You may also ask students to create their own word problems using their data and that of a classmate. Have students record their problems set in context and then pass the problems around, challenging their classmates to solve them.

2.3
Wii Hit the Waves

Game Used
Wii Sports Resort Wakeboarding

Common Core Math Standards
(2.NBT.1) Understand that the three digits of a three-digit number represent amounts of hundreds, tens, and ones; e.g., 706 equals 7 hundreds, 0 tens, and 6 ones. Understand the following as special cases:

- (2.NBT.1a) 100 can be thought of as a bundle of ten tens— called a "hundred."

- (2.NBT.1b) The numbers 100, 200, 300, 400, 500, 600, 700, 800, 900 refer to one, two, three, four, five, six, seven, eight, or nine hundreds (and 0 tens and 0 ones).

Description of Lesson/Activities
Begin the lesson by reviewing with students that a three-digit number such as 465 can be thought of in expanded form as addition of the place values (400 + 60 + 5, or 4 hundreds + 6 tens + 5 ones). Have a student volunteer to demonstrate Wakeboarding in front of the class as you review game controls and call

Balance Board Games

For some balance board games, when a light student plays and a heavier student follows, the controls will be too sensitive for the heavier student (or not sensitive enough when a lighter student follows a heavier one). To recalibrate, click on "Quit" rather than "Retry" when a round is complete.

attention to where the score is recorded. Record the final score in the public space and have students record the score in their math journals. As a class, determine what each digit represents in order to write the score in expanded form. Have students record this as a statement in their math journals beside the score (e.g., "815 equals 8 hundreds, 1 ten, and 5 ones, or 815 = 800 + 10 + 5").

As additional students participate, ask the class to analyze their data by answering questions such as the following:

- How many hundreds/tens/ones does the next score need to have in order to be greater than this score?

- If we subtracted 3 hundreds from this score, what number would we have left?

- What number is in between the scores of our last two participants?

- If we switched these digits around, what combination would make the largest number possible? The smallest?

2.4
Team Table Tennis

Game Used
Wii Sports Resort Table Tennis: Table Tennis Return

Common Core Math Standard
(2.NBT.6) Add up to four two-digit numbers using strategies based on place value and properties of operations.

Description of Lesson/Activities

Have students sit in groups of three or four and create a team name. Explain that today, teams will compete for the highest score by finding the sum of their individual scores in Table Tennis Return. Demonstrate game controls and point out that, while returning a ball earns the player one point, knocking over a soda can earns three bonus points. However, failing to return one ball in the game will result in the end of the player's turn. Select a team to go first and allow each team member to participate in one round of the game. Record scores in the public space as each student records the scores in their math journals. At the end of each team's turn, have students add all of the scores together to determine the team's total score. Repeat until all students have had the chance to participate and all team scores have been calculated. Throughout the game, ask questions such as the following:

- How many points does the next team need to score in order to be ahead of the current high-score holder?

- How many points would a team need to be in the lead by 50 points?

- What is the difference between two given teams' scores?

- What team had the greatest tens or ones place value?

2.5
Hula Hoop Differences

Game Used
Wii Fit Plus Aerobics: Hula Hoop

Common Core Math Standards
(2.NBT.1) Understand that the three digits of a three-digit number represent amounts of hundreds, tens, and ones; e.g., 706 equals 7 hundreds, 0 tens, and 6 ones. Understand the following as special cases:

- (2.NBT.1a) 100 can be thought of as a bundle of ten tens—called a "hundred."

- (2.NBT.1b) The numbers 100, 200, 300, 400, 500, 600, 700, 800, 900 refer to one, two, three, four, five, six, seven, eight, or nine hundreds (and 0 tens and 0 ones).

(2.NBT.3) Read and write numbers to 1000 using base-ten numerals, number names, and expanded form.

(2.NBT.4) Compare two three-digit numbers based on meanings of the hundreds, tens, and ones digits, using >, =, and < symbols to record the results of comparisons.

(2.NBT.7) Add and subtract within 1000, using concrete models or drawings and strategies based on place value, properties of operations, and/or the relationship between addition and subtraction; relate the strategy to a written method. Understand that in adding or subtracting three-digit numbers, one adds or subtracts hundreds and hundreds, tens and tens, ones and ones; and sometimes it is necessary to compose or decompose tens or hundreds.

Description of Lesson/Activities

Students alternate playing the game to generate a three-digit number. Spectators will record the number and represent it using a hundreds, tens, and ones place-value mat and base-ten blocks. Have students use a place-value and expanded-form recording sheet to record how many hundreds, tens, and ones are in each score. Ask students, "What is 10 more (or less) than your value?" and "What is 100 more (or less) than your value?" and "How do you know?" "How far is that number from the next (or previous) hundred?" or "If you counted by fives from that number, what is the next even number you would say?" Direct students to choose a student score to compare with a partner. Partners cannot choose the same student's score to compare. Once all students have taken their turn, direct them to a partner and ask them to compare their numbers using >, =, and < symbols to record the results of their comparisons. Ask students to find the difference and/or sums of their value and their partner's value. Prompt students to share their strategies. Students should also find the difference between their value and their partner's value. Ask students to record some other subtraction equations they can think of that subtract a hundreds or tens value from their value (example: 263 − 40 = 223 and 263 − 200 = 63). Allow them to use base-ten blocks or to solve the equations as appropriate.

2.6
Tightrope Walk Lengths

Game Used
Wii Fit Plus Balance Games: Tightrope Walk

Common Core Math Standard
(2.MD.5) Use addition and subtraction within 100 to solve word problems involving lengths that are given in the same units, e.g., by using drawings (such as drawings of rulers) and equations with a symbol for the unknown number to represent the problem.

Description of Lesson/Activities
Generate a word problem with students that reflects the situation of the game. For example, "Ellen was playing Wii Tightrope and she walked 67 yards in her turn and Matt walked 25 yards in his turn. How many total yards did Ellen and Matt walk on the tightrope?" Let students know that they will work with partners to solve the problems, inserting their names and scores for those of Ellen and Matt. Provide students with a variety of resources they can use to solve their problems, such as base-ten blocks, hundreds charts, and the like. For an extension, change the problem to include an unknown: "Kaitlin walked 46 yards on the tightrope. Together, she and her partner, Casey, walked 94 yards. How many yards did Casey walk on the tightrope?" Offer students part-part-whole mats and base-ten blocks or hundreds charts for solving the problem.

Spark 2.6
This lesson spark's alignment to CCSS 2.MD.5 is illustrated in Table 3.1, page 26.

Lesson Sparks for Intermediate Grades (3–5, Ages 8–11)

Students in intermediate grades are often well-versed in the use of technology, especially when it translates to gaming. When we work with such students, we often are greeted with a handful of kids trying to one-up their classmates by showing how skilled they are at the game selected for the day's lesson. Still, many students, whether they admit it or not, require support when it comes to modeling game mechanics in order to be successful on a given activity. While their hand-eye coordination is more advanced than most primary students, balance games and precision-movement games still offer a challenge.

Considering this, the following lesson sparks incorporate games students may already be familiar with, but approach the activities through the eyes of a mathematician. The lessons challenge students to see the math contained in their favorite sports and encourage students to draw deeper conclusions based on mastery of the math standards and their understanding of the world around them.

TABLE 4.4 Wii Games for Intermediate Grade Sparks 3.1–5.6

Grade	Wii Sports	Wii Sports Resort	Wii Fit Plus
3	3.1, 3.2	3.3, 3.4	3.5, 3.6
4	4.1, 4.2	4.3, 4.4	4.5, 4.6
5	5.1, 5.2	5.3	5.4, 5.5, 5.6

Third Grade Lessons (Ages 8–9)

3.1
Wii Control Our Multiplying

Game Used
Wii Sports Baseball (Training): Swing Control

Common Core Math Standard
(3.OA.7) Fluently multiply and divide within 100, using strategies such as the relationship between multiplication and division (e.g., knowing that $8 \times 5 = 40$, one knows $40 \div 5 = 8$) or properties of operations. By the end of Grade 3, know from memory all products of two one-digit numbers.

Description of Lesson/Activities
Display a dartboard and ask students to explain how scores vary depending on where a dart lands during a game. Students should reach the understanding that the closer a dart is to the center, or bull's-eye, of the dartboard, the greater the number of points earned. Explain that the game you will use today follows a similar scoring guideline: the closer a player hits a baseball toward the desired direction, the greater number of points he or she earns. Draw a table in the public space in order to tally scores as each student participates. The table should include five columns labeled *Dark Blue, Light Blue, White, Outside of Zone,* and *Miss.* Reveal the point values for each column (dark blue = 10 points, light blue = 6 points, white = 3 points, outside of zone = 1 point, miss = 0 points) and have students tally along with you in their math journals as a student volunteer completes one game of Swing Control. Determine the points earned for each column by multiplying the total tallies by the point value. Add the points together to calculate the student's total points and check the calculation against the score displayed on the Wii. Allow other students to participate while the class tallies and calculates points for each student's performance. Throughout the activity, ask questions such as the following:

- What is the highest score possible on Swing Control?

- What is the highest score a student could achieve while still getting at least one tally in each of the columns? The lowest score?

- What other combination of tallies would equal the same score as (a given student score)?

3.2
Wii Compare Power Throw Fractions

Game Used
Wii Sports Bowling (Training): Power Throws

Common Core Math Standards
(3.NF.1) Understand a fraction 1/b as the quantity formed by 1 part when a whole is partitioned into b equal parts; understand a fraction a/b as the quantity formed by a parts of size 1/b.

(3.NF.2) Understand a fraction as a number on the number line; represent fractions on a number line diagram.

Description of Lesson/Activities
Using a standard game of bowling on Wii Sports, bowl one frame and then ask students how the score could be represented as a fraction (e.g., 7 pins knocked down = 7/10). Have student volunteers explain what each digit in the fraction represents. The class should conclude that the numerator represents the number of pins knocked down and the denominator represents the total number of pins.

Using a number line beginning at 0 and extending to 1, with tenths marked, ask the class to determine where this fraction should be placed on the number line. Explain to students that today you will be using a bowling game where the number of pins to knock down increases in each frame. The class will compare the number of pins knocked down in each frame by using number lines. Have a student volunteer bowl the first frame on Power Throws. Ask students, "What number should we use in the denominator to represent the total number of pins in this frame?" and "What number should we use in the numerator to represent the number of pins knocked down?"

If using a number line in the public space, ask a student volunteer to record the score from the first frame as a fraction on the number line. If students are working independently, have each student complete his or her own number line, then discuss their answers. As the game progresses, a row of pins is added to each set of pins. You can discuss with the students what increments should be used to create the number line for each frame, or use the suggestions shown in Table 4.5.

TABLE 4.5 Power Throw Fraction Number Line Increments

Frame	Total no. of pins	Suggested increments for number line
1	10	increments of 2
2	15	increments of 3
3	21	increments of 3
4	28	increments of 4
5	36	increments of 6
6	45	increments of 9
7	55	increments of 11
8	66	increments of 11
9	78	increments of 6
10	91	increments of 13

<table>
<tr><td>

Web Help for Number Lines

You can create number-line handouts for your students using websites such as http://themathworksheetsite.com/numline.html.

</td></tr>
</table>

As your students progress through the frames, compare the number lines created for each frame, asking questions such as, "In which frame (select two) was a greater fraction of pins knocked down?" Or assign tasks such as, "List the frames (or pin fractions) in order from least to greatest fraction of pins knocked down."

3.3
Wii Multiply from the Three-Point Line

Game Used
Wii Sports Resort Basketball: 3-Point Contest

Common Core Math Standard
(3.OA.4) Determine the unknown whole number in a multiplication or division equation relating three whole numbers. *For example, determine the unknown number that makes the equation true in each of the equations $8 \times ? = 48$, $5 = \underline{\quad} \div 3$, $6 \times 6 = ?$*

Description of Lesson/Activities
As students enter the teaching space, display an image of a basketball court. Ask a student volunteer to explain the significance of the three-point line in basketball (any shot scored from behind this line earns the team three points as opposed to the standard two-point score). Have another student volunteer to model the 3-Point Contest game. At the end of his/her turn, ask the class, "What are the rules for the 3-Point Contest?" and "How many points does a player earn for each basket he/she makes?" In this game, every fifth ball counts as a bonus ball, earning the player two points if scored. Tell the class that, because this is a math class, today's game will be scored differently. Ignoring the game's scoring system, every basket

scored in today's game will be multiplied by a random multiplier. The multiplier will be determined by rolling one or (later) two dice. The sum of the numbers displayed on the dice will act as the multiplier for the participant's score. It's up to the class to determine how much the participant scored after each round. Prior to participating, have each student volunteer roll a die to determine the multiplier. Record the number in the public space. Following the player's turn, record the total number of baskets scored and ask, "What would this player's score be if each basket was worth ___ points?" As more students have a chance to participate, refrain from rolling multipliers. Rather, following the player's turn, provide the class with a sum based on the score and ask the class to determine the multiplier. To challenge students more, add a second die and have students combine the total for the dice to act as the multiplier of the given problem.

3.4
Beach Dog Graphing Fun

Game Used
Wii Sports Resort Frisbee: Frisbee Dog

Common Core Math Standard
(3.MD.3) Draw a scaled picture graph and a scaled bar graph to represent a data set with several categories. Solve one- and two-step "how many more" and "how many less" problems using information presented in scaled bar graphs. *For example, draw a bar graph in which each square in the bar graph might represent 5 pets.*

Description of Lesson/Activities
Have students sit in groups of three or four and create a team name. Explain that today, each team will create scaled bar graphs based on the results of the team members playing Frisbee Dog. Demonstrate game controls on the Wii or by using an actual Frisbee with the students. Modeling form will play a big role in students' success with this game. Ask a student volunteer to play five rounds (half a game) of Frisbee Dog, pointing out to the class the in-game scoring grid, where players can earn a greater number of points

by throwing the Frisbee closer to the center of the bull's-eye. As the player participates, tally the number of Frisbees caught in the pink, green, and yellow zones as well as those missed. With the help of the class, create a bar graph to represent the scoring results of the player. Explain that as teams compete, the numbers will be much higher in each category, so students will have to determine how to scale the bar graphs on their grid paper (such as one square represents two scores) in order to display the full data. Have students consider how the bar graph would change if 10 or 20 tallies were added to each category. Suggest creating a scale in which each square of the bar graph represents two scores. Modify the graph to reflect the new numbers, then prepare teams for the activity. Appoint a student to tally the scores of all the students in a given team to ensure that the information is recorded accurately. After the players in each team complete their turns, have the class create bar graphs of the team's data. In the end, each student will have completed several bar graphs that can be compared. Ask the class, "How many more scores in the pink zone did (Team 1) make compared to (Team 2)?" "How many fewer scores in the green zone did (Teams 1 and 2) combined make compared to (Teams 3 and 4) combined?" "Which team was the most successful at throwing the Frisbee into the bull's-eye?" "Which two teams' combined scores create an even-numbered sum?"

3.5
Ski Jump Rounding

Game Used
Wii Fit Plus Balance Games: Ski Jump

Common Core Math Standards
(3.NBT.1) Use place value understanding to round whole numbers to the nearest 10 or 100.

(3.NBT.2) Fluently add and subtract within 1000 using strategies and algorithms based on place value, properties of operations, and/or the relationship between addition and subtraction.

Description of Lesson/Activities

Students take turns generating scores by playing the game. As players take their turns, have the spectators record the score and represent the score on a number line. You may wish to model locating a score on a number line before asking students to work independently. After they plot the value on a number line, ask students to round it to the nearest 10 and 100. As students work, ask them questions such as, "How far is that number from the next (or previous) 10 (or 100)?" or "What is 10 (or 100) more (or less) than that number?" or "Is that number closer to ___ or ___ (use values such as 0, 50, 100, etc.)?" Once all students have taken their turn, direct them to a partner and ask them to find the sum of their value and their partner's value. Ask students to share their strategies. If time allows, ask students to work with a new partner, repeating the previous directions.

3.6
Heads Up—Soccer

Game Used
Wii Fit Plus Balance Games: Soccer Heading

Common Core Math Standards
(3.NBT.1) Use place value understanding to round whole numbers to the nearest 10 or 100.

(3.NBT.2) Fluently add and subtract within 1000 using strategies and algorithms based on place value, properties of operations, and/or the relationship between addition and subtraction.

Description of Lesson/Activities

Students alternate generating scores by heading the ball. As players take their turns, have the spectators record the scores as addition equations. For example, Player A scores ___ and Player B scores ___, so ___ + ___ = ? After students find the sum of two scores, ask them to find the difference. As students work, ask them questions such as, "If you rounded the two scores to the nearest 100, what would be their sum (or difference)?" or "Is that score closer to 0, 500, or 1000?" or "What would I need to add to that number to get a sum of 1000?" Ask students to share their strategies for solving the problems.

Fourth Grade Lesson Sparks (Ages 9–10)

4.1
Bowling Fractions to Decimals

Game Used
Wii Sports Bowling

Common Core Math Standard
(4.NF.6) Use decimal notation for fractions with denominators 10 or 100. *For example, rewrite 0.62 as 62/100; describe a length as 0.62 meters; locate 0.62 on a number line diagram.*

Description of Lesson/Activities
Students take turns bowling a frame. As players take their turns, have the spectators record one of the frame scores in the center of a Frayer Model recording sheet. Students will record the score as a fraction in the center and label each quadrant of the recording sheet with the following prompts: a drawing of the fraction, the fraction on a number line, the fraction in words, the fraction as part of a set. As students work, ask them questions such as, "Is that value closer to 0, ½, or 1?" or "What is the name of a fraction equivalent to that one?" or "How many more tenths would I need to add to that value to make 1?" Ask students to share their strategies for solving the problems.

4.2
Power Throws

Game Used
Wii Sports Bowling (Training): Power Throws

Common Core Math Standard
(4.OA.5) Generate a number or shape pattern that follows a given rule. Identify apparent features of the pattern that were not explicit in the rule itself. *For example, given the rule "Add 3" and the starting number 1, generate terms in the resulting sequence and observe that the terms appear to alternate between odd and even numbers. Explain informally why the numbers will continue to alternate in this way.*

Description of Lesson/Activities
Students take turns generating scores by bowling the ball. Before the player bowls, determine a rule, such as "add 6." As players take their turns, have the spectators record the score and follow the rule to generate the next five terms in a pattern. For example, if a player bowls a 7 on her first attempt, spectators will find the next five terms to be 13, 19, 25, 31, and 37. As students work, ask them questions such as, "What kinds of numbers are we getting each time we add?" or "If we continue to follow this rule, when will you get an even term?" or "What else do you notice?" and "How would it be different if the rule was add 5?" then "Why do you think the sums alternate between even and odd when the rule is adding an odd number, but this is not so when you add an even number repeatedly?" Ask students to explain their reasoning.

4.3
Geometry Speed Slice

Game Used
Wii Sports Resort Swordplay: Speed Slice

Common Core Math Standard
(4.G.1) Draw points, lines, line segments, rays, angles (right, acute, obtuse), and perpendicular and parallel lines. Identify these in two-dimensional figures.

Description of Lesson/Activities

In order to establish this activity, the class will play Speed Slice several times. Have two student volunteers play one game of Speed Slice while you draw a silhouette of one of the sliced objects. It is important to draw the image large enough so that it is clearly visible for all students. Have two new student volunteers play a game of Speed Slice, but first indicate to the class that you're going to watch closely in the game for the object you drew. When the object comes up, use a ruler to draw a line indicating the direction in which the object was sliced. Draw two points on the object: one where the blade entered and a second where it left. Label the points *A* and *B*. Ask a student to trace line segment *AB* with a finger, trace an invisible line parallel to line *AB*, or trace an invisible line segment perpendicular to line *AB*. Before starting the next game of Speed Slice, distribute a sheet of paper to each student and instruct them to draw the object they want to watch for. Explain to the class that whenever their object shows up in the game, they are to draw a line using a ruler to indicate which direction the object was sliced. Since everyone is drawing different objects, answers will vary.

During subsequent rounds of Speed Slice, students continue to watch for their object and draw a line indicating the slice. The result will be an object that is run through with several lines, some possibly intersecting and/or running parallel. Continue to label points and the blade's entrance and exit. After three or four rounds, begin asking students questions based on their drawings: "Who has a drawing with intersecting lines?" and "Who can name an angle created on their drawing by intersecting lines?" and "Does anyone have a right angle?" and "Can anyone show an obtuse angle in their drawing?" and "Which drawing has the longest line segment?" These answers can be recorded by students on a free space on their paper, discussed in small groups, or shared as a class using the public space or a document camera.

4.4
Wii Do Some Flips

Game Used
Wii Sports Resort Wakeboarding

Common Core Math Standard
(4.NBT.2) Read and write multi-digit whole numbers using base-ten numerals, number names, and expanded form. Compare two multi-digit numbers based on meanings of the digits in each place, using >, =, and < symbols to record the results of comparisons.

Description of Lesson/Activities
After demonstrating the game mechanics of Wakeboarding, provide each student with a lapboard or writing space and materials on which to write. Have two student volunteers each play a round of Wakeboarding and, following each round, have the class record the students' scores on his or her paper. For each score, have the class rewrite the number using standard form (e.g., 325), word form (e.g., 325 = three hundred twenty-five), and expanded form (e.g., 325 = 300 + 20 + 5). After both volunteers have taken a turn, have students compare the number using <, >, or =. Continue this practice through pairs of student volunteers as time allows, asking questions such as, "Which of these two scores has more tens?" and "How many more hundreds does (score A) have than (score B)?" For a fun extension, consider using a "Reverse Score Bracket" in which player scores are recorded in reverse (e.g., 325 becomes 523) on a score bracket and compete to knock one another out of the bracket until declaring a winner. This not only supports the standard, but also gives students a new set of numbers to work with, ones that the game does not automatically rank.

4.5
Swing-Analysis Conversion

Game Used
Wii Fit Plus Training Plus: Driving Range

Common Core Math Standard
(4.MD.1) Know relative sizes of measurement units within one system of units including km, m, cm; kg, g; lb, oz; l, ml; hr, min, sec. Within a single system of measurement, express measurements in a larger unit in terms of a smaller unit. Record measurement equivalents in a two-column table. *For example, know that 1 ft is 12 times as long as 1 in. Express the length of a 4 ft snake as 48 in. Generate a conversion table for feet and inches listing the number pairs (1, 12), (2, 24), (3, 36), …*

Description of Lesson/Activities

Students alternate taking a swing. As players take their turns, have the spectators record the score in a two-column table, performing the appropriate conversions. Offer students calculators as appropriate. For example, if Player A scores a distance of 28 yards, spectators will record the value in the table on their recording sheet, make the conversion, and record that in the table also. The table may look like the one in Table 4.6.

TABLE 4.6 Swing Analysis Conversion Table

Scored distance	
In yards	In feet
50	150
28	84

As students work, ask them questions such as, "How can we find that value in inches?" or "How do you know if you need to multiply or divide when converting?" or "What else can you think of that might be that length?" You may wish to provide calculators for some or all students. Ask students to share their strategies for solving the problems.

4.6
Snowball Fight!

Game Used
Wii Fit Plus Training Plus: Snowball Fight

Common Core Math Standard
(4.OA.4) Find all factor pairs for a whole number in the range 1–100. Recognize that a whole number is a multiple of each of its factors. Determine whether a given whole number in the range 1–100 is a multiple of a given one-digit number. Determine whether a given whole number in the range 1–100 is prime or composite.

Description of Lesson/Activities
Students alternate turns using the Wii. In this game a turn lasts 120 seconds, so fewer students will get a turn during the first class period. You may wish to schedule an additional class period to ensure equity. Begin by asking students, "Who can share a definition of a prime number with the class?" and "How about a composite number definition?" and "Given those definitions, how would we describe the number 1?"

During the game, pairs of spectators should have a laminated hundreds chart and a dry-erase marker and eraser. As the student player hits the targets, ask the spectators to follow along with their hundreds charts, marking prime numbers as the score increases. When the score is a composite number, ask students to record the number and its factors. When the player's turn ends, ask students to record the ending score in their journals. Students should determine whether the result is prime or composite. Pick a number (2–9), and ask student to determine whether the player's score is a multiple of that number. Ask students to share how they know or how they figured it out.

Fifth Grade Lesson Sparks (Ages 10–11)

5.1

Wii Convert Measurements

Game Used
Wii Sports Golf

Common Core Math Standard
(5.MD.1) Convert among different-sized standard measurement units within a given measurement system (e.g., convert 5 cm to 0.05 m), and use these conversions in solving multi-step, real world problems.

Description of Lesson/Activities

Allow students to take turns golfing a game. You may wish to limit the number of strokes a player takes in order to include more students (we recommend two or three strokes per student). Draw students' attention to the upper right-hand corner of the screen; the number of yards remaining to make it into the hole will appear after each stroke (as the golfer gets closer to the hole, it will appear as feet). While students are spectators, they should record this number on a sheet of paper, math journal, or small dry-erase board and convert it from yards to feet (or feet to yards, depending on which unit is displayed). Calculators may be used for the conversions. After a student completes their first stroke, ask students, "How many yards are left?" and "If we converted that to feet, would the resulting number be larger or smaller?" and "How would you calculate the number of feet remaining?"

Allow a few students to golf. Make sure students are recording the distance remaining and converting it to feet or yards. Ask students how the decimal form of the converted distance can be related to fractions, and how might that be calculated. For example, 112 feet = 37.33 yards. "What does the .33 (repeating decimal) mean?" or "Who knows an equivalent fraction to that decimal?" or "What does 1/3 of a yard mean?" or "What is the value of 1/3 of a yard?" You may wish to provide the students with yardsticks and standard rulers for this exploration.

5.2
Tennis

Game Used
Wii Sports Tennis

Common Core Math Standards
(5.NBT.3) Read, write, and compare decimals to thousandths.

- (5.NBT.3a) Read and write decimals to thousandths using base-ten numerals, number names, and expanded form, e.g., $347.392 = 3 \times 100 + 4 \times 10 + 7 \times 1 + 3 \times (1/10) + 9 \times (1/100) + 2 \times (1/1000)$.

- (5.NBT.3b) Compare two decimals to thousandths based on meanings of the digits in each place, using >, =, and < symbols to record the results of comparisons.

(5.NBT.4) Use place value understanding to round decimals to any place.

Description of Lesson/Activities

Welcome the class wearing a stopwatch on your person, or display in the public space an online stopwatch (such as the one available at www.online-stopwatch.com). Time the students and tell them how long it took the class to come into the room and be seated quietly. Record their time in the public space in thousandths, then round it to the nearest whole number. Ask if the class can improve their time by performing another task, such as getting out home-work, taking a seat at the front of the room, and so on. Again, time them and record the time in the public space. Round the time accordingly, asking for help from the students with the calculation. Explain that today we will be playing tennis and timing how long it takes to score from the time of the serve. They will have the oppor-tunity to record times against the computer and compare them to times competing against a classmate. Have two student volunteers model how to play the game for the rest of the class. After a few points have been scored, have a student use the stopwatch to record how long it takes from the time of the serve for a player to score. Record this score in the public space. As a class, round this number to the hundredths, tenths, and ones places. Repeat this process for several more scores, rounding the numbers and comparing the various scores to one another.

Once you are confident that students understand the day's activity, distribute writing materials and have students keep score of the times as others have the opportunity to volunteer. Have the timekeeper read aloud the time to the class using number names, and ask a second student volunteer to record the time in the public space as students record the score in their writing materials, checking for accuracy. Throughout the activity, support student inquiry by asking questions such as, "Which of these two scores is greater?" "What is an example of a number that is between these two given scores?" When given two scores with the same tens and ones place, ask, "Do you think it's necessary for stopwatches to record tenths/hundredths/thousandths of a second? Explain why."

5.3
Add and Compare Decimals

Game Used
Wii Sports Resort Bowling: 100 Pin

Common Core Math Standards
(5.NBT.3) Read, write, and compare decimals to thousandths.

- (5.NBT.3a) Read and write decimals to thousandths using base-ten numerals, number names, and expanded form, e.g., $347.392 = 3 \times 100 + 4 \times 10 + 7 \times 1 + 3 \times (1/10) + 9 \times (1/100) + 2 \times (1/1000)$.

- (5.NBT.3b) Compare two decimals to thousandths based on meanings of the digits in each place, using >, =, and < symbols to record the results of comparisons.

(5.NBT.7) Add, subtract, multiply, and divide decimals to hundredths, using concrete models or drawings and strategies based on place value, properties of operations, and/or the relationship between addition and subtraction; relate the strategy to a written method and explain the reasoning used.

Description of Lesson/Activities

In this lesson each student will get the opportunity to bowl a full frame (two throws). Seat students in groups of two to four per table. Make base-ten blocks available to students for finding the sum and for making comparisons. As a player bowls, the spectators record their scores as decimals and add the two throws. For example, if Player A knocks down 87 out of 100 pins in her first throw and 4 of the 100 in her follow-up throw, the spectators will record .87 + .04 = .91. Then they will represent the sum using expanded form. Each player will record their own total value on an index card. Once players have all had a turn, ask students to find a partner and compare their values using > and < symbols to record the results of their comparisons. If students are working at tables of four, ask them to order their decimals from least to greatest.

Locked Games

First-time users will find 100-Pin Bowling and other advanced Wii Sports and Wii Sports Resort games locked. Playing the standard game in the Bowling category will grant access to 100-Pin Bowling.

5.4
Slide into Expressions

Game Used
Wii Fit Plus Balance Games: Penguin Slide

Common Core Math Standards

(5.OA.1) Use parentheses, brackets, or braces in numerical expressions, and evaluate expressions with these symbols.

(5.OA.2) Write simple expressions that record calculations with numbers, and interpret numerical expressions without evaluating them. *For example, express the calculation "add 8 and 7, then multiply by 2" as $2 \times (8 + 7)$. Recognize that $3 \times (18932 + 921)$ is three times as large as $18932 + 921$, without having to calculate the indicated sum or product.*

Description of Lesson/Activities

Students will work in pairs for this lesson. Before calling students to play Penguin Slide, assign each pair of students a color of fish to tally: blue (1 point each), green (2 points each), or red (10 points each). As each student plays the game, make sure that the spectator partners are recording the number of times their partner catches the assigned color of fish. Once all players have taken a turn, ask students to express as a calculation the point value of their score combined with their partner's score. For example, if partners are recording green fish (2 points) and partner A catches 4 fish while partner B catches 3 fish, the calculation may read as follows: "Add 4 and 3, then multiply by 2" or $2 \times (4 + 3)$. If time allows, ask students to switch partners and repeat the task. Partners should exchange their calculations with another partnership that had a different color and evaluate their responses.

5.5
Wii Run (and Rise) to Determine Coordinates

Game Used
Wii Fit Plus Aerobics: Two-People Run

Common Core Math Standard
(5.G.1) Use a pair of perpendicular number lines, called axes, to define a coordinate system, with the intersection of the lines (the origin) arranged to coincide with the 0 on each line and a given point in the plane located by using an ordered pair of numbers, called its coordinates. Understand that the first number indicates how far to travel from the origin in the direction of one axis, and the second number indicates how far to travel in the direction of the second axis, with the convention that the names of the two axes and the coordinates correspond (e.g., x-axis and x-coordinate, y-axis and y-coordinate).

Description of Lesson/Activities

Explain to your students that today they will be exploring coordinates while going for a run. Model sets of coordinates on a graph by drawing two axes in the public space. Show students a pair of coordinates such as (3, 5) and explain that the first digit informs how far to move along the x-axis, or the *run* (left to right), while the second digit indicates how far to move along the y-axis, or the *rise* (down to up). Share that students will run in pairs, one student being responsible for the *run* and the other for the *rise*, all the while running along a rising path up Wuhu Mountain. Have two student volunteers run one round, demonstrating game controls and familiarizing students with the game. As the students run, draw the class's attention to the progress chart on the bottom of the screen. Eight markers indicate the progress of each player, represented with icons, along the track. Students will record progress during the following rounds as each race leader reaches a new marker. When the two student volunteers have finished their race, have them return to their seats and distribute graphing paper to the class.

Have each student create a pair of axes with 10 points (labeled 0 to 10) on each axis. Students will record coordinates in the space below the graph and will draw coordinates on the graph following each student pair's race. As the student pair begins the game, keep score as coordinates as the leader reaches each of the eight markers: you will record the score (how many markers each player has passed) as coordinates, for example, if player X reaches marker 3 while player Y has only passed marker 1, record the score as (3, 1). As the students record each coordinate on their paper, the teacher should record coordinates in the public space. Continue recording coordinates (eight total) until the winner completes the race. Have students then map the coordinates on their graphs. Have students consider what would the graph look like

- if student X never moved during the race?
- if student Y never moved?
- if students X and Y were tied for the entire race?

5.6
Wii Tilt into Improper Fractions

Game Used
Wii Fit Plus Training Plus: Tilt City

Common Core Math Standard
(5.NF.1) Add and subtract fractions with unlike denominators (including mixed numbers) by replacing given fractions with equivalent fractions in such a way as to produce an equivalent sum or difference of fractions with like denominators. *For example, 2/3 + 5/4 = 8/12 + 15/12 = 23/12. (In general, a/b + c/d = (ad + bc)/bd.)*

Description of Lesson/Activities
Divide the class into three teams and assign each team a color (yellow, red, or blue). Tell students that for the remainder of class this is their team color and encourage them to root for their team. Have a student volunteer demonstrate the game, and draw students' attention to the large marbles that fall during the round. Students will determine what fraction of marbles are scored for a given color. Provide each student with materials to write with and select a student to play the first round. While this student plays, the class should tally how many large marbles matching their color appear and, of those marbles, how many the player scores. (Note: There are five large marbles for each round in the Beginner level. The color of these marbles, however, is random.) After the end of the first round, have students each determine the fraction of marbles scored for their given color. Have a new student play a second round while the class keeps score. After students rewrite the new score as a fraction, ask the class to add the fractions from both rounds together to determine the fraction for both rounds combined. To provide an additional challenge, have students play at a more difficult level. While students play, ask the class, "What would the fraction look like if the player scored all of the marbles for a given color? None of the marbles?"

Lesson Sparks for Grades 6 and 7 (Ages 11–13 and GT Ages 9 and Up)

Gifted and talented (GT) or advanced academic programs exist in many schools throughout the country. In such programs, students typically encounter math concepts two years above the enrolled grade level. For example, a fourth grade student in GT math may quite possibly be learning concepts from the sixth grade Common Core Curriculum Standards. Students in our particular school district have the opportunity to take GT math in Grades 4 and 5. It is, in part, because of this that we have decided to include lessons for Grades 6 and 7 in this book.

Although the math standards become progressively more complex in later grade levels, numerous opportunities still exist to support mathematical concepts through the use of the Wii and the games incorporated in previous lessons. In particular, a number of our colleagues teaching at the middle-school level have adopted the Wii into their algebra instruction as both motivation to the students and as an instructional tool to support mathematical concept attainment.

TABLE 4.7 Wii Games for Grades 6 and 7 and GT, Sparks 6.1–7.6

Grade	Wii Sports	Wii Sports Resort	Wii Fit Plus
6	(not used)	6.1, 6.2, 6.3	6.4, 6.5, 6.6
7	(not used)	7.1	7.2, 7.3, 7.4, 7.5, 7.6

Sixth Grade Lesson Sparks
(Ages 11–12 and GT Ages 9 and Up)

6.1
Any Way You Slice It

Game Used
Wii Sports Resort Swordplay: Speed Slice

Common Core Math Standard
(6.RP.2) Understand the concept of a unit rate a/b associated with a ratio a:b with b ≠ 0, and use rate language in the context of a ratio relationship. *For example, "This recipe has a ratio of 3 cups of flour to 4 cups of sugar, so there is 3/4 cup of flour for each cup of sugar." "We paid $75 for 15 hamburgers, which is a rate of $5 per hamburger."*

Description of Lesson/Activities
Allow students to play the Speed Slice game and record a score. Ask students to gather several other student scores and record them in a data table. Using their data, pose questions such as, "If Ahnya scored 10 and Jonah scored 6, what would the ratio of Ahnya's score be to Jonah's?" and "If the ratio is 10:6, then what is the rate of Jonah's score in relationship to Ahnya's score?" (Jonah scores .6 of a point for every point Ahnya scores.) Provide time for students to practice the concept by making comparisons among other students' data. Give students the opportunity to find rates using their data and at least two other students' data.

6.2
Can You Canoe?

Game Used
Wii Sports Resort Canoeing: Speed Challenge

Common Core Math Standards
(6.RP.3) Use ratio and rate reasoning to solve real-world and mathematical problems, e.g., by reasoning about tables of equivalent ratios, tape diagrams, double number line diagrams, or equations.

- (6.RP.3a) Make tables of equivalent ratios relating quantities with whole-number measurements, find missing values in the tables, and plot the pairs of values on the coordinate plane. Use tables to compare ratios.

- (6.RP.3b) Solve unit rate problems including those involving unit pricing and constant speed. *For example, if it took 7 hours to mow 4 lawns, then at that rate, how many lawns could be mowed in 35 hours? At what rate were lawns being mowed?*

- (6.RP.3c) Find a percent of a quantity as a rate per 100 (e.g., 30% of a quantity means 30/100 times the quantity); solve problems involving finding the whole, given a part and the percent.

- (6.RP.3d) Use ratio reasoning to convert measurement units; manipulate and transform units appropriately when multiplying or dividing quantities.

Description of Lesson/Activities

Students take turns generating scores by playing the game. As other students take their turns, have the spectators record their score in their math journal. Once several students have had a turn generating a score, ask the students a question such as, "If you canoe 70.29 yards in one minute, how far would you expect to canoe in half an hour?" and "If you traveled at the same rate, what distance would you expect to travel in an hour?" Ask students to create a ratio table to record their findings. Provide calculators and other math tools as appropriate.

6.3
Factor in Bowling

Game Used
Wii Sports Resort Bowling: 100-Pin Game

Common Core Math Standard
(6.NS.4) Find the greatest common factor of two whole numbers less than or equal to 100 and the least common multiple of two whole numbers less than or equal to 12. Use the distributive property to express a sum of two whole numbers 1–100 with a common factor as a multiple of a sum of two whole numbers with no common factor. *For example, express 36 + 8 as 4 (9 + 2). Apply and extend previous understandings of numbers to the system of rational numbers.*

Description of Lesson/Activities

Students take turns generating numbers by bowling a frame. Direct students to write their number on an index card and list all of the factors. Once all students have generated a number and have their card, arrange students in groups of four. Ask students to find the greatest common factor (GCF) for their own number and then find the GCF for each of their group members' numbers, four GCFs in all. This information can be recorded in journals or on looseleaf paper. Ask students to partner with one other person from their group of four whose number had a common factor and use the distributive property to express a sum of two whole numbers between 1 and 100 with a common factor as a multiple of a sum of two whole numbers with no common factor. For example, if one score was 64 and another was 88, the pair would record $64 + 88 = 152$ as $8 (8 + 11) = 152$. Provide assistance as appropriate, asking students questions such as, "What other numbers from your group have a factor in common with one of your factors?" and "How might you express the sum using the distributive property?"

6.4
Heads to Misses

Game Used
Wii Fit Plus Balance Games: Soccer Heading

Common Core Math Standard
(6.RP.1) Understand the concept of a ratio and use ratio language to describe a ratio relationship between two quantities. *For example, "The ratio of wings to beaks in the bird house at the zoo was 2:1, because for every 2 wings there was 1 beak." "For every vote candidate A received, candidate C received nearly three votes."*

Description of Lesson/Activities

Assign students to cooperative groups with three members in each group. One person from each group takes a turn at the game. The second group member records the number of times the player heads the ball, while the third group member records the number of misses. The group will then find the ratio of heads to misses, expressing the value in ratio form and recording it on an index card. After all the groups have a value recorded, display the values for all to see. Ask students, "What do you notice about the values?" "What can we determine based on the ratios displayed?" "Which value is closest to 1:1 (or 2:1 or 1:3, etc.)?"

6.5
Ski Jump Box Plots

Game Used
Wii Fit Plus Balance Games: Ski Jump

Common Core Math Standards
(6.SP.4) Display numerical data in plots on a number line, including dot plots, histograms, and box plots.

(6.SP.5) Summarize numerical data sets in relation to their context, such as by:

- (6.SP.5a) Reporting the number of observations.

- (6.SP.5b) Describing the nature of the attribute under investigation, including how it was measured and its units of measurement.

- (6.SP.5c) Giving quantitative measures of center (median and/or mean) and variability (interquartile range and/or mean absolute deviation), as well as describing any overall pattern and any striking deviations from the overall pattern with reference to the context in which the data were gathered.

- (6.SP.5d) Relating the choice of measures of center and variability to the shape of the data distribution and the context in which the data were gathered.

Description of Lesson/Activities
Students take turns generating scores by playing the game. As other students take their turns, have the spectators record their score in their math journal. After at least ten students have had a turn generating a score, ask the students to create a box plot using the data. Allow students to work in partnerships to create their

graphical representations. Ask students to relate the quantitative measures of data, such as the median and mean, as well as the measures of variability, such as the interquartile range. Challenge partnerships to create an alternative graph of the data and compare the two representations. Spark a class dialogue about the pros and cons of each representation by asking, "What are some positive observations that you have about each representation?" and "What are some of the drawbacks for each representation?"

6.6
Slide into Ratios

Game Used
Wii Fit Plus Balance Games: Penguin Slide

Common Core Math Standard
(6.RP.3) Use ratio and rate reasoning to solve real-world and mathematical problems, e.g., by reasoning about tables of equivalent ratios, tape diagrams, double number line diagrams, or equations.

Description of Lesson/Activities
Before calling students to play Penguin Slide, ask students to set up a table to record how many of each colored fish each of the participants score. The table should include a column for each of the three colors of fish: blue, green, and red. Have students create a new row with each new participant. As each student plays the game, make sure that the spectators are filling in and extending the table. After each player has a turn, ask students, "What ratios do you see from the table?" and "What observations do you make about the ratios?" and "Find the percent of a red fish caught as a rate per 100." Challenge students by asking, "If you catch 7 blue fish for every green fish, then at that rate, how many green fish would you catch if you snagged 35 blue fish?"

Seventh Grade Lesson Sparks
(Ages 12–13 and GT Ages 9 and Up)

7.1
R U on Par?

Game Used
Wii Sports Resort Golf (Three Holes)

Common Core Math Standards
(7.NS.1) Apply and extend previous understandings of addition and subtraction to add and subtract rational numbers; represent addition and subtraction on a horizontal or vertical number line diagram.

- (7.NS.1a) Describe situations in which opposite quantities combine to make 0. *For example, a hydrogen atom has 0 charge because its two constituents are oppositely charged.*

- (7.NS.1b) Understand $p + q$ as the number located a distance $|q|$ from p, in the positive or negative direction depending on whether q is positive or negative. Show that a number and its opposite have a sum of 0 (are additive inverses). Interpret sums of rational numbers by describing real-world contexts.

- (7.NS.1c) Understand subtraction of rational numbers as adding the additive inverse, $p - q = p + (-q)$. Show that the distance between two rational numbers on the number line is the absolute value of their difference, and apply this principle in real-world contexts.

- (7.NS.1d) Apply properties of operations as strategies to add and subtract rational numbers.

Description of Lesson/Activities
Provide students with tools such as number lines and two-colored counter chips. Before students take their turns, ask them each to set up a table in which to record their data. An example of a table may look like Table 4.8.

TABLE 4.8 Tracking Data for Wii Golf Scores

| | Hole | | | |
	1	2	3	Total
Par				
Player's score				-
Difference (Player – Par)				

While the game is intended to be played by a single player, you may wish to set students up in teams of three so more students get the opportunity to take a turn golfing. As students take turns remind them to record their data in their table, noting the difference above or below par as a positive or negative number. As discussion points arise, ask students to discuss the distance from zero or the distance between the rational numbers of the player's score and par. Allow students to use the number lines or counters to make sense of these ideas. Ask students, "Were there any instances where the player's score and par were equal numbers?" and "If so, what does that mean for the score (or the difference)?" and "How does that relate to the idea of zero pairs?" and "If a player is 1 over a 4-par hole, they would have taken 5 swings to get the ball into the hole. What would their score be for that hole?" (+1) or "What if the player was 1 under a 3-par hole; what would their score be?" (–1).

7.2
Comparing Ski Jumps

Game Used
Wii Fit Plus Balance Games: Ski Jump

Common Core Math Standards
(7.SP.1) Understand that statistics can be used to gain information about a population by examining a sample of the population; generalizations about a population from a sample are valid only if the sample is representative of that population. Understand that random sampling tends to produce representative samples and support valid inferences.

(7.SP.2) Use data from a random sample to draw inferences about a population with an unknown characteristic of interest. Generate multiple samples (or simulated samples) of the same size to gauge the variation in estimates or predictions. *For example, estimate the mean word length in a book by randomly sampling words from the book; predict the winner of a school election based on randomly sampled survey data. Gauge how far off the estimate or prediction might be.*

Description of Lesson/Activities

For this lesson you will need two sets of data, so you may wish to split the class into two equally numbered groups. Another option would be to use the data from another class. If you choose the latter option, you will want the number of data points to be equal. Before students take their jumps, ask them to make a prediction about whose mean will be greater, their group's or the other group's. They should justify this prediction in some way. Students take turns generating scores by playing the game. As other students take their turns, have the spectators record their score in a table. You may wish to keep track of the data yourself in a table that you can later project for the whole class to see. After all students have had a turn generating a score, ask the students to create a double-dot plot using the data from both groups (this is where you may wish to project your data table so students can check theirs for accuracy). Allow students to work in partnerships to create their graphical representations. Ask students to relate the quantitative measures of data, such as the median and mean. Challenge partnerships to make statements about their graphs after they analyze them. Spark a class dialogue about the pros and cons of this representation by asking, "What are some positive observations that you have about this representation?" and "What are some of the drawbacks for this representation?" and "Which group actually had the greater mean and how did that compare with your earlier prediction?" and "What general statement(s) can you make based on the data?"

7.3

Eye on Percent Error

Game Used

Wii Fit Plus Training Plus: Bird's-Eye Bull's-Eye

Common Core Math Standard

(7.RP.3) Use proportional relationships to solve multistep ratio and percent problems. Examples: simple interest, tax, markups and markdowns, gratuities and commissions, fees, percent increase and decrease, percent error.

Description of Lesson/Activities

Inform students that the score for this game is measured by how far you fly (in yards) in one minute. Based on this information, ask them to make an estimate for their score. Students will need to record their estimate before they take their turns. After students take a turn, they will need to record their actual score. Now, walk them through finding the percent error using the formula:

$$\frac{|\text{Estimate Value} - \text{Exact Value}|}{|\text{Exact Value}|} \times 100$$

You may wish to review the symbolic representation for absolute value and discuss the meaning before asking students to calculate their percent error. Make calculators available to students as appropriate. Once students have found their percent errors, discuss some of the different values and what they mean. For example, ask, "If one student's percent error was 22% and another student's was 11%, what can you say about the percent errors?" and "What do those values mean?" and "What can be said about their estimates compared to their actual scores?"

7.4
The Tightrope Rates

Game Used
Wii Fit Plus Balance Games: Tightrope Walk

Common Core Math Standard
(7.RP.1) Compute unit rates associated with ratios of fractions, including ratios of lengths, areas and other quantities measured in like or different units. *For example, if a person walks 1/2 mile in each 1/4 hour, compute the unit rate as the complex fraction ½ / ¼ miles per hour, equivalently 2 miles per hour.*

Description of Lesson/Activities
Appoint a student (or rotate the job among several students) as the timekeeper. This student will need a timer. Have students record player data in a table such as the one shown in Table 4.9:

TABLE 4.9 Computing Unit Rates with Wii Tightrope Walk Data

Player name	Distance traveled (yards)	Time (minutes)	Rate (distance/time)

As players take their turns, the timekeeper times them. You need someone to do this job because the game will not display the time if the player does not make it all the way across the tightrope. In such a case, the score is how far the player traveled. It is very difficult to make it all the way across, so most players will get a score in yards. Ask students to calculate the rate at which the player traveled the rope. If the student was only on for a small number of seconds, then the student will convert their time (to the nearest hundredth) to a fraction of a minute. Provide calculators as appropriate. After all players have had their turns, discuss the meaning of the rates among the students by asking, "Who was the fastest tightrope walker?" "How far did that player go?" "Is there any relationship between how fast the player walks and how far he/she travels?" "What other statements can you make based on the rates displayed?" and "What strategy might you apply for the next time you play this game to increase your score?"

7.5
Combinations of Ten

Game Used
Wii Fit Plus Training Plus: Perfect 10

Common Core Math Standards
(7.NS.1) Apply and extend previous understandings of addition and subtraction to add and subtract rational numbers; represent addition and subtraction on a horizontal or vertical number line diagram.

- (7.NS.1a) Describe situations in which opposite quantities combine to make 0. *For example, a hydrogen atom has 0 charge because its two constituents are oppositely charged.*

- (7.NS.1b) Understand $p + q$ as the number located a distance $|q|$ from p, in the positive or negative direction depending on whether q is positive or negative. Show that a number and its opposite have a sum of 0 (are additive inverses). Interpret sums of rational numbers by describing real-world contexts.

- (7.NS.1c) Understand subtraction of rational numbers as adding the additive inverse, $p - q = p + (-q)$. Show that the distance between two rational numbers on the number line is the absolute value of their difference, and apply this principle in real-world contexts.

- (7.NS.1d) Apply properties of operations as strategies to add and subtract rational numbers.

Description of Lesson/Activities
Players take turns playing the game to make ten. As the player correctly hits the addends to make ten, the game will introduce the player's ability to use three addends and negative numbers.

When other students take their turns, have the spectators represent their equations using a number line or two-colored counters. Ask students to accurately record their equations using a number-line diagram. Provide assistance as appropriate to any students struggling with representing their equations using the number-line diagram.

7.6
Bubbling Equations

Game Used
Wii Fit Plus Balance Games: Balance Bubble

Common Core Math Standards
(7.EE.4) Use variables to represent quantities in a real-world or mathematical problem, and construct simple equations and inequalities to solve problems by reasoning about the quantities.

- (7.EE.4a) Solve word problems leading to equations of the form $px + q = r$ and $p(x + q) = r$, where p, q, and r are specific rational numbers. Solve equations of these forms fluently. Compare an algebraic solution to an arithmetic solution, identifying the sequence of the operations used in each approach. *For example, the perimeter of a rectangle is 54 cm. Its length is 6 cm. What is its width?*

Description of Lesson/Activities
Before students play the game, pose the following question to the students: "If a player went 996 yards, how many feet would the player have traveled?" and "What other information do we need to know to be able to solve for the unknown (the distance in feet) in this problem?" Record their responses, including those such as "Just multiply the distance in yards by 3, because there are 3 feet in a yard." Prompt students to generate an equation, using a variable for the unknown, such as $1/3x = 996$. Now, have students take turns generating distances by playing the Balance Bubble game. Ask each student to record the player's distance. Then, ask students to generate an equation that can be solved to find the distance in feet.

Ask students to compare the algebraic solution to the arithmetic solution and discuss their ideas. Facilitate the discussion to lead students to make connections between the algebraic solutions and the arithmetic solutions.

PART III

Wii SETUP
AND COMMUNITIES

As a planet, we spend 3 billion hours a week playing video and computer games. What elements of gaming can we harness for educational purposes?

The Gamification of Education infographic:
www.knewton.com/gamification-education

Acquiring a Wii for Your School:
What You Need and How to Get It

Budgets are tight. This is true of any school in any district, county, or state. And, let's face it, spending a couple hundred dollars on a video-game system is not likely to be approved by your principal, department facilitator, or PTA without strong convincing and hard evidence. But when times are tough, the tough get creative!

There are any number of untapped resources in your school and community that can greatly reduce the cost of bringing gaming technology into your school. You just have to know where to look and how to ask.

A Tale of Two Wii Consoles

As fate would have it, the Nintendo Wii came to each of our schools through very different means.

Meg's Wii found her at the end of a National Council of Teachers of Mathematics (NCTM) conference. As she tells it, Meg had no intention of heading out to the car amid the buckets of rain pouring on the parking lot, so she made her way to the auditorium and joined a smattering of conference attendees for the door prize drawings. Winners were taking home some pretty cool math manipulatives, but Meg was having no luck at all. Before long the final prize was announced: a Nintendo Wii console bundle. The prize seemed a little unusual for a math conference but, with a handful of kids at home, she thought it would be a pretty cool gift to win. The announcer read off the numbers of the winning ticket: the same numbers matching those on her ticket stub. Overcome with excitement, she ran down the aisle, claimed her prize, and immediately began to ponder a critical question: what connection does the Wii have to mathematics instruction? Meg kept this question in mind over the next several months as she sought to uncover how using the Wii in a classroom setting could actually support math instruction.

Matthew's Wii found him through a failed recycling drive and a successful donation campaign. As part of the recycling program at his school, Matthew's school community earns money for each ton of paper it collects. To maximize their earnings, the school's Green Team runs several paper drives throughout the year, increasing the amount of paper collected and, thereby, increasing the amount earned for the school. When the school's Positive Behavioral Interventions and Supports (PBIS) committee sought new venues to celebrate student success, Matthew suggested that they use the profits from the paper drives to purchase a Wii for the school. Classes could hold monthly Wii parties to celebrate those students who met the behavioral goals for the month.

Unfortunately, despite impressive recycling efforts, the fiscal payoff for recycling was not nearly enough to purchase a Wii and accessories for the school. But as luck would have it, a representative from an insurance agency was in the staff lounge to promote a donor site that schools could use to purchase much-needed equipment for classrooms. Matthew created a profile through the donor site and, with the approval of his principal, completed an online application requesting that donors purchase a Wii console, detailing why it was needed and how it could be used to support instruction within the school. The school community responded in a big way. Within four weeks, pledges from anonymous donors enabled the school to purchase two Wii console bundles, along with additional controllers and accessories. Matthew was determined to use the Wii systems as instructional tools within the school building. His new goal was to change (and challenge) the way teachers thought about delivering instruction.

If There's a Will, There's a Wii

As we will soon illustrate, there are many, many ways to bring gaming technology into your school. Some methods require little to no work on your part. Others will take hours of campaigning and defense of the technology as an instructional tool. But the most important and, perhaps, most difficult barrier to overcome is that of changing the culture in your school to one that believes in and supports the use of gaming technology.

On the surface, bringing a Wii into your classroom could easily look like the students are just playing video games in lieu of instruction, prompting questions such as the ones on the next page.

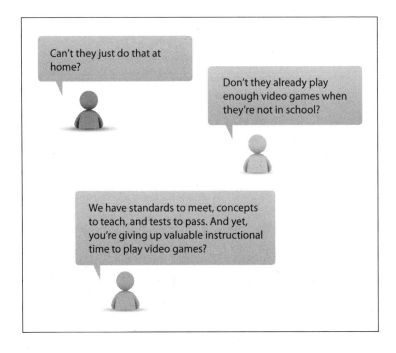

Effective use of the gaming technology hinges upon teaching practices that are evidence-based and instructionally valid. This calls for educators to be transparent when they discuss how they intend to include the tool in the classroom setting. Skeptics can be convinced of the tool's strength through evidence of well-planned lessons, good questioning, and students engaged in learning.

This is where **you** come into play:

You—who are well-versed in the language and interests of children.

You—who can name things that motivate your students without belaboring the thought.

You—who seek new ways to engage your students and help them to recognize the presence of mathematics in every facet of their world.

You motivate your students by identifying their interests and making meaningful connections to those interests throughout your instruction. You know that making content relevant to students is as important as teaching the skill itself. You delight in the *Aha!* moments: those times when a concept finally clicks for a student and when he or she is able to feel successful within a unit of study.

The Wii will not teach students mathematics; that is and will continue to be the role of the teacher. However, using the Wii as a tool to support math instruction is both highly motivating and highly effective. Your role as a facilitator of mathematics curriculum and instruction will definitely get more exciting for you, too, as you witness first-hand the higher levels of engagement and interest from your students.

Your students *could* just use the Wii at home, but if you use it as an instructional tool in your classroom, the mathematics emerging in the games they play will become obvious and accessible to them.

Your students probably *do* play enough video games outside of school, but if you model how to understand math concepts through game play, they can show what they learned to their parents and, potentially, use the home console to continue to work toward mastery of those concepts.

We *most certainly do* have standards to meet, objectives to teach, and tests to pass, but now you have another tool that can be employed to help students achieve these high standards.

Methods for Procuring a Wii for Your Classroom or School

Before bringing the Wii to your school, secure the appropriate approvals from your administration or school system. This technology is not on the approved purchase list for every school out there, so if it is not on your approved list, you can begin that process. The Wii was not on our district's list when we wanted to begin using the gaming technology, but through a few simple steps, we were able to get the device on our county's approved purchase list and begin engaging our students in meaningful, active learning.

If the only thing standing between you and bringing gaming technology into your classroom is the fiscal means to purchase a console, we hope the following resources and ideas will help you overcome that obstacle. Find the method that is best-suited for your school's population, budget, or circumstances. Start small by procuring one Wii console for use in a pilot classroom, or be more ambitious and purchase several consoles for use throughout the school building. Regardless, find what works best for you.

Bring in Your Wii from Home

This is most certainly the fastest way to test-drive the tool with students, albeit any damage caused to your console would be

Meg's Mii

your own loss. One thing to remember when bringing your console from home is making sure that all content on the Wii is appropriate for viewing by school-age children. Mii's, the name attributed to avatars created on the Wii, should be culturally respectful in name and design, such as these we designed of ourselves.

Matthew's Mii

Mentally review how you want the Wii to be viewed by colleagues and parents in your building, then make the appropriate decisions about what content you have loaded onto the console before using it with students. You will also want to be sure that this technology is on your school system's approved list before bringing it into your school. Find out who the contact is for list-approval in your area and make the appropriate inquiry. In our case, we initiated this in order to have the device reviewed and approved for use.

Allocate Monies from a Supplemental Budget

Does your school sponsor a book fair or other fundraiser? Do you have input on what purchases are made through the school's technology or AV budget? Does your school receive Title I funding? Is there funding for instructional materials? While cash flow to purchase materials and technologies is likely limited, those making budget decisions consistently look for purchases that will have the greatest effect in the school. Presenting a new technology tool such as the Wii, with the impact it could have on supporting instruction in a wide number of classrooms throughout the building, may be just the kind of investment they are seeking.

Appeal to Your Parent-Teacher Association

As with supplemental budgets, your school's PTA is not only a great source for support in funding a project, it's also a fantastic platform for advocating to parents about a new technology tool for your school. If possible, contact a PTA board member to demonstrate how you intend to use the console. Remember to ask potential stakeholders, such as PE teachers and alternative-education teachers, for input on how they might use the system in their instruction. This will help you build the strongest case possible to convince those who will be funding the project. Get on a PTA meeting agenda to pitch the idea to the PTA and any parents or educators who may be in attendance. Again, a demonstration of student learning is a very powerful tool in swaying others' opinions about the use of gaming in the classroom. With the release of the Wii U console, it is also possible that some families in the PTA or school community at large will wish to donate their Wii console for use in the school. Both the games and the hardware from the Wii are compatible with the new console. Consider a live demonstration of a student or several students using the Wii, or at least show a video of a lesson. You may also wish to supply some of the lesson sparks included in this book as planning evidence.

Seek Donations through Charity Organizations

Charity-driven websites such as DonorsChoose.org can be great sources of funding when looking to purchase new materials for the school. In fact, Matthew's school community purchased two Wii consoles that included Wii Sports and Wii Sports Resort with additional controllers in a matter of days, thanks to donations from community members through a project he listed on DonorsChoose.org. Pledges are made anonymously, and the materials are purchased and shipped after the project is fully funded. The ability to donate as little as a dollar made it possible for a great number of families to help purchase the Wii consoles for Matthew's school and also gave the school community a sense of ownership in the new technologies being used to support instruction throughout the building.

Inquire about Corporate Donations

Companies like to donate to schools. It is an easy way for them to demonstrate their support of education and it creates great public relations for the company. Corporate interest in philanthropic endeavors can certainly benefit you and your school. Why not seek out a donation of a Wii console from a local business, especially one that has an employee with a student at your school? View the company's charity policies online or visit the office and speak to a representative or store manager about donations and what steps you may need to take to get going on the right path.

Apply for a Grant

There are so many opportunities for writing grants. Some companies hold an annual grant competition to encourage educators who are excited about what they do and who bring unique learning opportunities into their classroom. These companies focus resources on education programs and partnerships, especially in the science, technology, engineering, and mathematics (STEM) areas. Supporting STEM initiatives is critical for their business and for national competitiveness, so they embrace programs that they think will help build a diverse employee pipeline.

Gear Up for Gaming

Determining the number of consoles to purchase is largely dependent on the size of your school and the interest you have built in support of the gaming technology. It is not necessary to invest a lot to make this a successful technology tool in your school, but you will want to consider purchasing the following items in order to make the most out of the content and suggestions in this book:

- **Wii Console with Wii Sports and Wii Sports Resort "Pak"**—Includes the Wii console, one MotionPlus controller, one nunchuk controller, one Wii Sports game disc, and one Wii Sports Resort game disc (retail $150.00).

- **Wii Fit Plus with Balance Board**—Includes Wii Fit balance board plus one Wii Fit Plus game disc (retail $99.99).

- **Wii MotionPlus Controller**—It is important to note that, while it is possible to play Wii Sports and Wii Fit Plus with a standard Wii controller, the MotionPlus is required to play the Wii Sports Resort games. Purchase at lease one additional Wii MotionPlus controller to support multi-player games (retail $25.00).

- **Wii Nunchuk Controller**—Purchase at lease one additional Wii nunchuk controller to support multiplayer games (retail $19.99).

- **Dual Charging Station with Two Rechargeable Replacement Batteries**—Wii controllers require two AA batteries each. These batteries provide approximately 25 hours of use. Switching to rechargeable batteries and a charging station can save the school lot of money (retail $24.99).

- **Rechargeable Battery Pack for Wii Fit Balance Board**— The Wii Fit balance board requires four AA batteries, providing approximately 60 hours of use. A rechargeable battery pack that recharges using a USB cable can be purchased for the Wii Fit balance board (retail $4.99).

- **Wii Travel Bag**—A carrying case is a good investment to transport the Wii console, accessories, and game discs from class to class. Most Wii travel bags can store the console, up to four controllers and nunchuks, and several game discs (retail $12.99).

- **Wii U hardware**—Purchasing a Wii U console is not necessary for using this book. Both the 8GB white console (retail $299.99) and the 32GB black console (retail $349.99) come with a sensor bar. These units also come with a Wii U GamePad and GamePad stylus. They do not come with any games. Nor do they come with any Wii remotes.

The cost will depend largely on whether you decide to purchase a new console or find a well-maintained used system. Pricing also varies depending on the venue from which you purchase the system. Retail pricing will be fairly consistent from store to store, but using a donor site such as DonorsChoose.org may result in a slight mark-up in cost in order for the third-party vendor to cover operating costs.

Determine where you will store the console and accessories once they arrive at your school and develop a way to inventory the materials so that you can maintain all components in working order and track usage of the console throughout the building. You may be the only one using the tool at first, but we can say with confidence that it will catch on very quickly. We have successfully used a wiki to track sign-out and return of the technology at our school, although there are many different ways to track its use.

Set Up for Success

If you have a Wii at home, setting the console up at school will not be that different, aside from considering a much larger audience. The following tips will help make your first experience a success.

- **Connect the Wii to an LCD projector.** Use a 3 RCA composite audio/visual cable (the one with yellow, white, and red prongs) to connect your Wii console to an LCD projector. Your console will come with this cable, as do most LCD projectors. Connecting to an LCD projector will allow for a much larger projection. Your LCD projector should also allow for sound output. Check the LCD menu to make sure the speakers are enabled and turned up loud enough for the students to hear.

- **Secure space for participants to move.** Students will want to avoid getting whacked with a remote. It's a good idea to designate a space for students using the Wii that is a safe distance away from observers. It's also good to make sure players aren't standing too close to the projector cart during their turn. Despite having the rubber protective sleeve on our Wii remotes, our students still sometimes smack the controller against the cart when moving a little too energetically in response to the game.

- **Be thoughtful when positioning the sensor bar.** The Wii console utilizes wireless remotes that communicate to a sensor bar placed somewhere in the vicinity of the television or screen. Placing this sensor bar too near the ground in relation to the screen will force your participants to aim lower in order to get the sensor bar to pick up the signals from the remote. This isn't a problem when using a television, because one typically places the sensor bar on top of the stand holding the TV. However, when using a projector and screen it is best to place the sensor bar on a raised surface, such as a chair or AV cart, in order to bring it as close to the bottom of the screen as possible.

- **Consider your student groupings.** Sometimes it is beneficial to group students so that some rotate through the Wii station, while others engage in a related activity. You may wish to use a two- or three-group model, depending on the learning styles and behaviors of your students. If you have another adult in the room, you may want them to facilitate one group while you work with the Wii group. Don't be surprised, though, if they ask to take a turn with the group using the Wii!

If You've Got It, Flaunt It!

By bringing the Wii into your classroom, you are playing a part in changing the culture of your school. And as with any change, in a school or otherwise, there will be skeptics.

Your first experience using the Wii with your students will be memorable for many reasons. The students will be excited beyond words, perhaps even perplexed and amazed that a teacher would offer the chance to play video games in school. But for the students, this is the carrot they're willing to chase endlessly in order to do something so out of the ordinary in the classroom setting. As for you, this experience could be filled with excitement, anxiety, trepidation, and doubt as you try something completely new with your class.

We faced these questions ourselves (see the next page) when we used the Wii in school for the first time. Furthermore, when sharing this information with other professionals, we still hear questions such as these. However, you can anticipate and respond to these questions before you use the device in the classroom, because they revolve around communicating instructionally sound teaching practices.

If you are anxious about using the technology and managing your students simultaneously, try to get someone who has used the device to co-teach with you the first time you use the Wii. In our experience, it is helpful if you have a definite plan for your role and your co-teacher's role. For example, you might be the one to assist students with beginning a new round in the sport used for your activity, providing the participating student with support on game technique as well as giving the class cues for recording data for the lesson activity. This allows your co-teacher to circulate throughout the class and provide support to the students as they record their scores and solve the problems posed.

If your circumstance does not support opportunities for co-teaching, find comfort in the fact that you have a classroom full of experts who will gladly troubleshoot any problems that may arise. Those problems will seem insignificant compared to the fun you and your students will have with the lesson.

Top Four Troubleshooting Tips

Here is a list of the most common dilemmas we run into while using the Wii in our classrooms.

TIP 1
Batteries

The batteries in the Wii remotes certainly won't last forever, especially not after a hard day of gaming. We've recommended purchasing rechargeable battery packs, but that doesn't eliminate the issue of dealing with a dead battery.

What to look for: Watch for a blinking blue light on the Wii remote, which indicates the battery is nearly out of power. Another easy way to check battery life is to press the "Home" button while the Wii is turned on. A Wii remote icon will display at the bottom of the screen, indicating how much battery life remains.

How to avoid a problem: If using AA batteries, removing batteries from the remote after use will prolong their life. Alkaline batteries last longer, but cost more than standard AA batteries. If using rechargeable battery packs, make sure to charge the packs before using the system.

TIP 2
Sensor Bar

In order for the wireless remotes to work, the signal must be picked up by the sensor bar. The sensor bar connects to the Wii from a very thin wire and, as the Wii console set-up instructions indicate, should be placed in front of or below the screen onto which you are projecting. If the sensor bar is knocked to the floor or bumped so that it is no longer facing forward, the sensitivity of the cursor's movement will be compromised.

What to look for: Do students need to aim the Wii remote at an unusual angle in order for the cursor to appear on screen? If so, then the location of the sensor bar needs to be adjusted so that the direction in which the Wii remote is pointing directly corresponds to the position of the cursor on screen. If it doesn't, the issue lies with the placement of the sensor bar.

How to avoid a problem: Make students aware of where both the sensor bar and the wire connecting it to the Wii are located. If possible, conceal the wire so that a student could not trip over it. In addition, the sensor bar can be taped to a surface to prevent further movement.

TIP 3
Unlocked Games

Wii Sports and Wii Sports Resort each contain a number of games that are not available for play initially. Unlocking each game typically entails playing the game before it in the category. For example, to access the 100-Pin Game in Wii Sports Resort Bowling, you must first play the standard game in the Bowling category. If your school has more than one Wii console, you will have to unlock the games on each console. Fortunately, each game only needs to be unlocked once. You need not worry about the effects of unplugging or moving the system.

Wii Fit Plus also calls for some planning and preparation before your first use with students. Specifically, Wii Fit Plus requires that you create an account the first time you use it with a Wii console.

What to look for: Check the Wii Sports or Wii Sports Resort menu for the specific activity you plan to use prior to working with your students. If you have not yet unlocked the game, the game's title will not appear in the category menu.

How to avoid a problem: When you first use Wii Sports or Wii Sports Resort, unlock all the games at once. This will give you a feel for all of the games available on the disc, and you'll save yourself time in the future.

TIP 4
Wii Fit Plus Balance Board

The Wii Fit Plus balance board calibrates to the user's mass, making the sensitivity of the controls vary from student to student. While this may not matter in all games, it will certainly be evident in a number of them. If the system is not recalibrated in a given game between turns of students, the results can be frustrating.

Picture a seesaw, then imagine that a rabbit and a golden retriever each wants to take turns riding on the seesaw. What happens if the rabbit gets on first, and then the retriever gets on? What if the retriever is first to get on, followed by the rabbit?

This analogy applies to the Wii Fit Plus balance board. If a light student plays and a heavier student follows, the controls will be too sensitive for the heavier student. On the other hand, if a heavier student is followed by a light student, the controls will not be sensitive enough for the light student.

What to look for: If movement of the avatar is choppy or not responding to the student's movement, the Wii Fit Plus balance board is not calibrated correctly for the participating student.

How to avoid a problem: When a round is complete, click on "Quit" rather than "Retry." Retrying maintains the calibration from the previous student; quitting allows the board to recalibrate as the new student steps onto it.

If You Have It, They Will Play

Bringing the Wii into the school is the easy part. Advocating for its use among classroom teachers throughout the building is a more daunting task. In each of our schools, we started small, using the Wii with our own students, seizing the interest of curious teachers, and promoting technology use to those most willing to try something new.

As with any grassroots movement, building a strong foundation for adoption (in this case of a new technology tool) is the most effective means for achieving acceptance. What was once seen as a great incentive for positive behavior or an enticing reward to students working to earn a lunch bunch and Wii recess has evolved into a widely embraced practice. Now teachers and students alike reap the numerous rewards of using the Wii as an instructional tool in the math classroom.

Organizing a Wii PLC or Family Event

Extending use of the Nintendo Wii beyond your classroom is not only a great way to advocate for the tool, it's also an effective means of building support within your building and throughout the school community.

We have used both professional learning communities (PLCs) and after-school events to promote use of the Wii in our schools. Each method lends itself to supporting students in various ways, and both require significant time commitments in order to be successful. Finding what works best for you can lead to increased support from teachers, administrators, and parents, as well as additional funding toward the purchase of more technology.

Both Wii PLCs and Wii Family and Math events are described below, but are by no means the only effective methods. Feel free to adapt what we lay out below based on your resources and your school's needs.

Wii-Centered Professional Learning Communities

Many schools make use of professional learning communities (PLCs) to support instruction and deliver professional development. In a PLC, each member has something to offer and many come from a variety of experience levels and backgrounds. The common goal of the PLC often focuses on a specific instructional tool or approach, and members contribute time and talent to develop resources that support the tool in their classrooms or throughout the school. Participating members work collaboratively, seeking and sharing learning and then acting on that learning. A universal goal for the PLC members is to enhance their effectiveness as professionals for the benefit of their students.

Wii PLC at Matthew's School

Our Wii PLC meets every two weeks to explore ways the Wii can be used to support upcoming math instruction in our participants' classrooms. The nature of the PLC has evolved since its inception, but the focus remains the same. At the start, I asked each participant to complete a survey rating their comfort level with the Common Core Standards for Mathematical Practice and with using the Wii. Our school's transition to the Common Core challenged instruction throughout our building. I saw this as an opportunity to expand the tools we used to support mathematics instruction. Understandably, many educators placed a greater priority on familiarizing themselves with the Common Core. Fortunately, we universally agreed on the goal of familiarizing ourselves with the Standards for Mathematical Practice and the CCSSM, using the Wii as a vehicle to drive our interactions with the practices and standards.

FORM 6.1 Comfort Level with CCSSM and Wii

Survey Questions

On a scale of 1–10, where would you rank ...

... your current personal experience with using the Wii? _____

... your current knowledge of the Common Core Math Practices and Standards? _____

... your current experience with using the Wii in the classroom setting? _____

... your comfort level incorporating the Wii into math instruction? _____

On a scale of 1–10, to what degree do you believe gaming technology can be used effectively as an instructional tool? _____

Comfort with the Wii

The survey results of our seven PLC members indicated that, despite varied experience with using the Wii, most members were comfortable enough to try it in their math classrooms. This may not be surprising, given that these teachers voluntarily joined the Wii PLC.

Familiarity with Common Core

What was more interesting to me, however, was that the majority of participants indicated that their knowledge of the Common

Core was at the most basic level (ranks scoring 1–3). This informed me that a greater emphasis needed to be placed on familiarizing teachers with the mathematical standards for their grade levels while the PLC explored how to support these standards by using the Wii in the classroom.

And so our PLC began meeting every other Monday. I set up the Wii in the library media center's teaching area and laid out copies of the Common Core State Standards for Mathematics for teachers to use as a reference while brainstorming lessons. Our participants spent the majority of the time familiarizing themselves with how each game is played and where the math exists in the game itself. I asked participants what concepts their students would be exploring over the next two weeks and then demonstrated some games that could be used to support their lessons. If the standard involved adding single-digit numbers with a sum no greater than 20, I asked myself, "What game displays single-digit numbers or results in single-digit scores that could be added?" If the standard called for students to determine the factors of a number no greater than 100, I asked, "What game produces a two-digit score that varies with each participant and can be used to determine factors?"

With time, our roles in the PLC shifted. Teachers began to see their own connections to the CCSSM, developing lessons using the Wii based on the needs of their students and their own instructional agendas. As one teacher actively used the gaming technology in his class, others on that grade-level team were eager to follow. Of course, seeing the students get excited about the technology and be eager to use it over and over did not hurt either.

Wii Family Events

Students are a powerful tool in any marketing campaign.

Want to increase attendance at the school's annual Spring Fair?

Have students create posters and commercials advertising the games and events featured at the fair.

Want to raise funds for a charitable cause?

Have students create a movie showcasing their thoughts on the cause and how others can help.

Want to see the Wii used more frequently or in more classrooms throughout the building?

Simply stated: If it involves student learning, get students involved!

Choose Your Own Adventure (or Three Wii Nights Families Will Love!)

After-school and evening events can take many different shapes and require massive coordination and volunteer support, depending on the scale and the community's response to the event. Below you will find a walkthrough of how we have planned and carried out successful events using the Wii, from conceptualizing the evening to ensuring you have secured enough resources to provide maximum participation by your attendees.

You may wish to start out with a smaller event to gain a better handle on how to run the evening, what troubleshooting issues might arise, and what kind of interest the event will draw from your school community. This is certainly a case where you can easily bite off more than you can chew. Feel free to adapt the three Wii-centered evening events we describe below to meet the needs of your students, staff, and school community and to make these events successful at your school.

EXAMPLE 1
Boys' (or Girls') Night Out

At this evening event, sons and dads (or significant male figures) participate in activities that emphasize teamwork and building relationships. Activities vary at this annual event, but the Wii has been a big hit. Wii systems are set up throughout the school building and teams of five to six father/son pairs compete against other teams for high scores on a given game. The scores are broadcast via an interactive Google Doc (see pp. 124–125, Step 6) so participants can see in real time how other teams are doing. A similar event was also offered at Girls' Night Out and received a great response. Opportunities to connect with math occurred most frequently when discussing the range of scores represented throughout the teams and how many more points a given team needed to take the lead position.

EXAMPLE 2
Wii Family Competition

Taking the idea of competition one step further and promoting the family unit (even if participants are not directly related), the Wii Family Competition challenges participants in several different games. Each family member competes in a single event, and the family with the highest cumulative score receives the first-place ribbon. Because a number of different games are played simultaneously throughout the school building, this event requires a greater amount of coordination. Opportunities for math abound: there are as many math connections as there are different games being played, if not more. One effective way of connecting activities to the Common Core Math standards is to have fact and

Family-Night Posters

Hang fact and quiz posters near stations to

- connect the activity with Common Core standards
- give participants waiting for a turn something to do
- challenge participants

quiz posters hanging at or near each station, and challenge participants to think critically about the math application each activity holds.

EXAMPLE 3
Wii Math Night

Like the Wii Family Competition, a Wii Math Night features a variety of games for both children and adults. The difference in this case is that the Wii Math Night has clear, intentional connections between math concepts and the activities set up for participants. This event is a great advocacy tool to communicate to parents and teachers the effectiveness of using the Wii as an instructional device. It's also an opportunity to model how parents can help support their child's math skills at home with similar activities (video games accompanied by math-based questions).

Eight Steps to a Successful Wii Night

One key to coordinating a successful event is to make sure it is well-planned and well-thought-out. Below is a sequence I have followed to make our Wii Math Night a hit.

STEP 1
Book a Date in Advance

Your first step to success in holding the Wii family game night will be to meet with the administration to set a date. This date should be put on the school calendar immediately and sent home to parents. Doing this will make it easier for everyone involved with planning other activities at your school to know dates that are already reserved. As you plan, make sure to focus on publicity. Do anything you can to get people to overcome math anxiety for the night and enjoy learning as a family.

In addition, be sure to reserve the locations in the school where family game night will be held. For example, if it is in your school gym, you need to make sure that no sporting activities are scheduled to be using the gym. If you're going to be using classrooms, check ahead of time with the teachers. If classroom furniture needs to be moved, request a seating chart diagram so that things can be put back in order for the following school day.

STEP 2
Recruit Team Members

Once you have established that you are committed to holding a family game night on a certain date, you need to begin to build the team of educators and volunteers that will help out with the evening and its organization. Essential team members include an administrator, classroom teachers, and parents.

An administrator can help with developing your vision for the event and coordinating resources to make the event a success. He or she can ensure that no other events conflict with yours, and can also be vital in recruiting teacher volunteers.

Teachers are crucial to this event. They represent how instruction is being delivered in the classroom and are often the first person families recognize. Teachers can be strong advocates for the technology, and having a teacher run a station at your event may even inspire the teacher to use the technology more frequently in his or her classroom.

Parents also play a key role in coordinating these events. If you need additional Wii consoles, parents can help secure the technology from other families in the community. Choosing parents who are active in the school community can even result in some positive PR, as outspoken parents are often excited to share innovative and motivating things happening within the school building. Having support for the event from the PTA can also translate to additional resources such as help in acquiring door prizes from local businesses, food for volunteers, and extra advertising to increase attendance.

These events would fall apart without a few good people lending their time and talents, so make an effort to reward your volunteers in some way. We all know that evening sessions such as a game night make for a long day. Many businesses are willing to provide prizes for the volunteers who are helping out; all you need to do is ask.

Each volunteer will take on different responsibilities for the evening. You will want to make clear exactly what those expectations are, so each person understands his/ her part and is empowered to complete their end of the bargain efficiently. It is helpful to set a timeline for completing each task that will go into running this evening smoothly. Thankfully, so many of the details and specifics can be handled through emails, so it is not necessary to hold a lot of meetings surrounding the event.

STEP 3
Consider the Essential Questions

As you are considering the night, think about what your goal is for the evening.

- Do you have a specific theme or focus in mind for the event?

- Is your goal to increase the number of attendees at a particular event?

- Is your goal to increase community awareness about the use of technology in the school?

- Will you focus on playing games with students and parents that stimulate learning and communication?

- Will you have in place some form of communication between the educators and the families about the games and activities chosen?

- Are you using this event as a bridge between the community and the school, thereby making more parents feel at ease in and informed about the learning environment?

- Do you plan to send home ideas for continued interaction and extended learning at home?

Perhaps your response will be "all of the above," and that is fantastic because planning and implementing an interactive family game night using the Wii will accomplish all of those objectives plus the goal of having fun and spending quality time together.

When you have determined the focus for your event, advertise it! Let others throughout the building and district know what great activities you have planned for your school community and give them a chance to get involved. If you hold a specialty position in the school, alert your supervisors and colleagues from other schools. Perhaps they have attended or hosted similar events and have wisdom to share that will to make your event more successful. They may even volunteer to help on the day of the event.

STEP 4
Planning within the Physical Space

After setting your goals, it is time to develop a timeline for acquiring resources and to begin thinking about the school layout and where you might set up the learning stations.

Consider the following questions to inform your decisions:

How many participants do you anticipate?

Use an interest survey or data from similar past events to help estimate how many may attend your event.

Are parents also encouraged to participate?

If your activities are student-centered but you plan to encourage parent participation, plan accordingly. Participant numbers double when both students and parents are involved in activities.

Will your stations be open or scheduled?

If participants travel freely from one station to another, you may consider how you will handle disproportionate lines at the stations. If participants travel from station to station within an assigned schedule, consider how you will determine which station each participant visits.

You can determine the number of Wii consoles needed based on your answer to these questions. Games on Wii Sports, Wii Sports Resort, and Wii Fit Plus last on average between one and two minutes. If you take into consideration the number of participants, a group of 15 should each be able to have a turn at a station during a 30-minute session.

If your event draws 150–200 participants, setting up a minimum of ten Wii consoles can assure participation from the maximum number of attendees. Spreading out the Wii consoles, such as in separate classrooms or throughout the building, will provide the much-needed space for your attendees to move around safely while playing the games.

Consider what your participants will do while waiting their turn. One suggestion is to hang posters with questions (e.g., trivia questions) and facts (e.g., Common Core standards being addressed) related to the game.

The volunteer running the station can also ask trivia-style questions relating to the activity (such as when the sport was first played), to math (such as identifying the mean score of the participants so far or the difference between the highest and the lowest score), or to the Wii (like how many Wii consoles have been sold worldwide or what the first Nintendo game was).

Sample trivia questions:

- How many calories would a participant burn in an hour of doing the activity?

- When did the sport become an Olympic event (if applicable)?

- What records are held in the given sport and by what individuals?

If a large crowd is expected, extra stations might be included, such as calculator math, math read-alouds, online math gaming centers, or other materials that might support your theme for the evening. While planning the event, consider who will be responsible for creating these questions, who will assist students as they make calculations, and what tools are needed (pencils, paper, calculators, manipulatives, etc.) at each station.

When you have determined the scope of resources needed for the event, create a timeline for yourself and the others involved in the planning to ensure all of the materials are collected on time. Table 6.1 illustrates a sample timeline.

TABLE 6.1 Sample Timeline for Wii Night

3 months before event	Schedule event on school calendar; begin recruiting teachers and volunteers; hold first meeting to share vision of event.
2 months before event	Contact local businesses about donations for door prizes.
6 weeks before event	Send home flyer advertising event with a "save the date" notice.
4 weeks before event	Send home with all students a sign-up flyer advertising event, with tear-off RSVP; determine how many Wii consoles and what games are needed for the event; email teachers and parents requesting to borrow equipment.
3 weeks before event	Determine what classrooms and/or building space will be used during event; contact classroom teachers if their rooms will be used.
2 weeks before event	Deadline for families to turn in sign-up form. (Note: forms will still trickle in.)
1 week before event	Teachers/parents bring in Nintendo Wii consoles and drop off at designated location; if your event will feature an assigned schedule, assign students/families to groups and create personalized schedules to be distributed at the registration table on the night of the event.
1–3 days before event	Prepare materials for the stations, including any posters or additional supplies needed; distribute copies of the evening schedule as well as directions for the station to any volunteers.
Night of event	Set up equipment and rooms; test equipment and have a back-up plan should something not work; clean up and return materials following the event.

STEP 5
Determining the Length of the Event

Another important decision is the time during which the event will take place. Prior to setting any details, such as when sessions will occur or how long each will last, you must first determine what time of day the event will take place. Holding it too early in the evening may conflict with parent work schedules or family dinner plans. If the event is too long you may risk losing the interest of your participants. Often our evening events are from 6:00–8:30 p.m. This allows time for registration, which is an important opportunity to welcome families and distribute any pertinent information, and still provides plenty of activity time throughout the remainder of the evening.

We typically include the following information in the packets handed out at registration:

- schedule for the evening
- map of the school with stations marked
- brief description of the evening's activities and connections to math
- raffle tickets (if having a door-prize drawing)
- feedback form (collected at the end of the event)

You may also wish to keep track of the parents and students that attend your event. This information can be collected on the tear-off RSVP form sent home in advance to advertise the event, or it can be collected at the registration table. We've offered special prizes to the best-represented homeroom, which often helps to boost attendance to the event.

STEP 6
Keeping Score

If high scores play a role in any of your activities, find a cool way to share them with the attendees and fellow volunteers. One way we

accomplished this was through the use of a Google Doc. Anyone
with a Gmail account has access to Google's collaborative Drive
website, in which any number of users can interact on the same
document simultaneously. We used one such document to broadcast our high scores throughout the building. Using a desktop
or laptop set up near each station and connected to the online
Google Doc, our volunteers updated the high score as participants
came through their station, creating a live feed of high scores for
all attendees to see. Many volunteers projected these scores onto
a classroom wall or simply left the computer in a location easily
viewed by the attendees. Students and parents crowded around
the screen regularly to see what new high scores were recorded
throughout the building before rushing off to those stations in an
attempt to set a high score of their own.

The result was an easy-to-update, anonymous, captivating score-
board with real-time information to impress our attendees.

STEP 7
Door Prizes for Event Kick-Off and Closing

Many communities like to have an opening and/or closing gath-
ering so the educators can thank the community for coming out,
address some of the highlights of the evening, hold a raffle, and
collect feedback from the evening. It is a great idea to invite an
administrator to share some opening or closing remarks in addition to circulating from station to station throughout the evening.

Another idea that our participants have enjoyed is to assign a
volunteer the role of event photographer. His or her job is to take
pictures chronicling the event, then compile the photos into a
slideshow to share with attendees at the close of the event. Students
may catch a glimpse of themselves or their friends playing at a
station. Parents may see some great shots of their whole family
having a great time. Teachers can be reminded of the success of the
event and check out what other volunteers were doing throughout
the building. But best of all, everyone can witness how much fun

the community shared during this evening. Making these pictures available to include in the school yearbooks is certainly an added bonus, and it gives students and their families a chance to look back at the end of the year and remember what a great time they had at the Wii Game Night!

STEP 8
Contact the Press

It is often said that educators do not broadcast their successes enough. We work tirelessly to host memorable events for our students and community, seldom asking for any more attention than witnessing a happy reaction from a student. However, there's much to be said for drumming up some positive public relations for your school.

Contact the local newspaper, news station, or government official and let them know about your upcoming event. The worst that could happen is that they will say they are unable to attend. In contrast, when your school makes the front page of the local newspaper for showing how video games are reaching a new class of learners, you can revel in the well-earned praise for your school and staff.

Finding What Works for You

As mentioned previously, leading a Wii PLC or coordinating a Wii-centered after-school event can build support for the Wii as an instructional technology tool and motivate teachers who are considering using the Wii in their classrooms. By enlisting teachers, recruiting volunteers, and expanding outreach to the school community, you are building a network of support that will not only increase the effectiveness of using the Wii in your classroom, but will also benefit countless students within your school building. And it can all be as simple as finding what works best for you.

Forming a
Wii Instructional Network

One of the most affirming aspects of working in education is the willingness of colleagues to share ideas, collaborate on new projects, and challenge the ways we approach educational practices in order to provide the very best learning environment for our students. Our work with colleagues has spurred new Wii math lesson ideas and has helped us to better support teachers incorporating video games into their instructional practice for the first time.

When we first started using the Nintendo Wii in our schools, we struggled to find instructional content online from other educators working with the Wii. Many resources supported using the Wii in physical education classes, most often incorporating the Wii Fit Plus game and balance board to promote strong exercise habits. Few websites or journal articles examined the instructional impact of the Wii, and fewer still were explicit in exactly how Wii games could be incorporated as a tool in the math classroom. This is not to say that educators aren't thinking about how a tool as familiar to students as video games could be harnessed to support education in their classrooms. Rather, we saw a need to establish a home base of sorts, where educators could share their ideas freely and a collection of free resources could be amassed.

If You Build It ...

Our Wiki—A Living Document

And so we established the Wii Instructional Network, a wiki built to house teacher-created lessons and materials for using the Wii in the math classroom. The wiki can be viewed at http://wiilearning. wikispaces.com. Anyone can request membership in order to add to or edit the site's content. Our vision is for the Wii Instructional Network to become what this book cannot: a living document whose lessons and materials become the work of a community and whose content reflects the needs of the community of educators who are using it the most.

Educational Standards

CCSS for Math. If educators find new games to support the Common Core State Standards in Math, we hope the network will be reflective of those new titles.

CCSS for ELA. And if teachers incorporate experiences of using the Wii with students into their English, ELL, or language arts instruction, we hope those teachers will find a home for their ideas and resources in this instructional network.

NETS for Students. Likewise, we also hope educators will be mindful of ISTE's National Educational Technology Standards (NETS) for Students, as we were when developing the lesson sparks contained in this book (Appendix C).

As the needs of our community evolve, so, too, can the Wii Instructional Network, to support educators who are incorporating video games into their daily practice as an effective instructional tool.

This book only scratches the surface of the possibilities of using the Wii to support math instruction. The real bounty, we hope, will be found on the Wii Instructional Network as educators create and contribute what they're using in order to better serve students in schools throughout the world. We have already populated the wiki with lessons not included in this book. We purposefully excluded the lessons in this book so that the instructional network will provide a balance to what we shared here. The Wii Instructional Network contains mostly bare-bones lesson outlines that include the name of the game, the Common Core Standard addressed, and a bulleted list of the steps involved in the activity. Some lessons were created in collaboration with colleagues, and others are the products of brainstorming how a given standard could be supported through a Wii game.

Wii Need Your Help

With the Wii Instructional Network in place, we hope to be joined by educators like you as we tread new ground in instructional practice and look toward new ways the Wii can be used to support

Join Us!

Wii Instructional Network
http://wiilearning.wikispaces.com

learning in the math classroom. The more each of us shares—whether by creating new lessons and posting them to the wiki, sharing materials such as student handouts, or even posting the presentations you made to your staff or district when you introduced them to the idea of using the Wii as a math tool—the more supportive an infrastructure we'll be able to build.

All of this translates to an opportunity to pioneer a new educational frontier together and to make connections along the way that will support and enhance your instruction and the instruction of others.

We sincerely hope you'll join us at http://wiilearning.wikispaces.com and help us to build a resource others can use to impact instruction in schools and illuminate the role video games such as the Wii can play in the math classroom.

APPENDIX

Correlation of Wii Lesson Sparks and Common Core State Standards

When working with the Common Core State Standards for Mathematics (CCSSM), it is helpful for teachers to have a firm understanding of the domains and standards. CCSSM offers a web page on how to read the grade-level standards (www.corestandards. org/Math/Content/introduction/how-to-read-the-grade-level-standards) that includes this definition for the terms *standards* and *domains*:

Standards define what students should understand and be able to do.

Domains are larger groups of related standards. Standards from different domains may sometimes be closely related.

Common Core Domains

The domains addressed by lesson sparks in this book are **boldfaced** in the following text. To identify the specific standards addressed by the lesson sparks, refer to Tables A.1–A.3.

Grade K Common Core State Standards include the following domains:

- **Counting and Cardinality (CC)**

- **Operations and Algebraic Thinking (OA)**

- Number and Operations in Base Ten (NBT)

- Measurement and Data (MD)

- **Geometry (G)**

- Mathematical Practices (MP)

Grade K lesson sparks address standards in the domains of Counting and Cardinality (CC), Operations and Algebraic Thinking (OA), and Geometry (G). For instance, K.CC.1 and K.CC.2 are addressed in Spark K.6; K.OA.4 is addressed in Spark K.1; and K.G.1 is addressed in Spark K.3.

Grade 1 Common Core State Standards include the following domains:

- **Operations and Algebraic Thinking (OA)**

- **Number and Operations in Base Ten (NBT)**

- Measurement and Data (MD)

- Geometry (G)

Grade 1 lesson sparks address standards in the domains of Operations and Algebraic Thinking (OA) and Number and Operations in Base Ten (NBT).

Grade 2 Common Core State Standards include the following domains:

- **Operations and Algebraic Thinking (OA)**
- **Number and Operations in Base Ten (NBT)**
- **Measurement and Data (MD)**
- Geometry (G)

Grade 2 lesson sparks address standards in the domains of Operations and Algebraic Thinking (OA), Number and Operations in Base Ten (NBT), and Measurement and Data (MD).

Grade 3 Common Core State Standards include the following domains:

- **Operations and Algebraic Thinking (OA)**
- **Number and Operations in Base Ten (NBT)**
- **Number and Operations—Fractions (NF)**
- **Measurement and Data (MD)**
- Geometry (G)

Grade 3 lesson sparks address standards in the domains of Operations and Algebraic Thinking (OA), Number and Operations in Base Ten (NBT), Number and Operations—Fractions (NF), and Measurement and Data (MD).

Grade 4 Common Core State Standards include the following domains:

- **Operations and Algebraic Thinking (OA)**
- **Number and Operations in Base Ten (NBT)**
- **Number and Operations—Fractions (NF)**
- **Measurement and Data (MD)**
- **Geometry (G)**

Grade 4 lesson sparks address standards in the domains of Operations and Algebraic Thinking (OA), Number and Operations in Base Ten (NBT), Number and Operations—Fractions (NF), Measurement and Data (MD), and Geometry (G).

Grade 5 Common Core State Standards include the following domains:

- **Operations and Algebraic Thinking (OA)**
- **Number and Operations in Base Ten (NBT)**
- **Number and Operations—Fractions (NF)**
- **Measurement and Data (MD)**
- **Geometry (G)**

Grade 5 lesson sparks address standards in the domains of Operations and Algebraic Thinking (OA), Number and Operations in Base Ten (NBT), Number and Operations—Fractions (NF), Measurement and Data (MD), and Geometry (G).

Grade 6 Common Core State Standards include the following domains:

- **Ratios and Proportional Relationships (RP)**
- **The Number System (NS)**
- Expressions and Equations (EE)
- Geometry (G)
- **Statistics and Probability (SP)**

Grade 6 lesson sparks address standards in the domains of Ratios and Proportional Relationships (RP), the Number System (NS), and Statistics and Probability (SP).

Grade 7 Common Core State Standards include the following domains:

- **Ratios and Proportional Relationships (RP)**
- **The Number System (NS)**
- **Expressions and Equations (EE)**
- Geometry (G)
- **Statistics and Probability (SP)**

Grade 7 lesson sparks address standards in the domains of Ratios and Proportional Relationships (RP), the Number System (NS), Expressions and Equations (EE), and Statistics and Probability (SP).

Lesson Spark Correlations

The correlation between the Common Core State Standards and the 48 lesson sparks in this book are summarized in Tables A.1–A.3.

TABLE A.1 Correlation of Lesson Sparks K–2 and CCSS Mathematics

	Grade K		Grade 1		Grade 2	
Domain	Standard	Spark	Standard	Spark	Standard	Spark
CC	K.CC.1 & K.CC.2	Spark K.6				
	K.CC.7	Spark K.2				
OA	K.OA.3	Spark K.4 & K.5	1.OA.1	Spark 1.1	2.OA.1	Spark 2.2
	K.OA.4	Spark K.1				
NBT			1.NBT.2	Spark 1.4 & 1.5	2.NBT.1	Spark 2.3 & 2.5
			1.NBT.3	Spark 1.3, 1.5, & 1.6	2.NBT.3, 2.NBT.4, & 2.NBT.7	Spark 2.5
			1.NBT.4	Spark 1.6	2.NBT.5 & 2.NBT.7	Spark 2.1
			1.NBT.5	Spark 1.2 & 1.5	2.NBT.6	Spark 2.4
			1.NBT.6	Spark 1.5		
MD					2.MD.5*	Spark 2.6*
					2.MD.10	Spark 2.1
G	K.G.1	Spark K.3				

*Spark 2.6, which addresses Grade 2 standard 2.MD.5, is illustrated further in Chapter 3, Table 3.1: Evidence of the Eight Practices within a Wii Math Lesson.

TABLE A.2 Correlation of Lesson Sparks 3–5 and CCSS Mathematics

Domain	Grade 3		Grade 4		Grade 5	
	Standard	Spark	Standard	Spark	Standard	Spark
OA	3.OA.4	Spark 3.3	4.OA.4	Spark 4.6	5.OA.1 & 5.OA.2	Spark 5.4
	3.OA.7	Spark 3.1	4.OA.5	Spark 4.2		
NBT	3.NBT.1 & 3.NBT.2	Spark 3.5 & 3.6	4.NBT.2	Spark 4.4	5.NBT.3 & 5.NBT.4	Spark 5.2
					5.NBT.3 & 5.NBT.7	Spark 5.3
MD	3.MD.3	Spark 3.4	4.MD.1	Spark 4.5	5.MD.1	Spark 5.1
G			4.G.1	Spark 4.3	5.G.1	Spark 5.5
NF	3.NF.1 & 3.NF.2	Spark 3.2	4.NF.6	Spark 4.1	5.NF.1	Spark 5.6

TABLE A.3 Correlation of Lesson Sparks 6–7 and CCSS Mathematics

Domain	Grade 6		Grade 7	
	Standard	Spark	Standard	Spark
RP	6.RP.1	Spark 6.4	7.RP.1	Spark 7.4
	6.RP.2	Spark 6.1	7.RP.3	Spark 7.3
	6.RP.3	Spark 6.2 & 6.6		
NS	6.NS.4	Spark 6.3	7.NS.1	Spark 7.1 & 7.5
EE			7.EE.4	Spark 7.6
SP	6.SP.4 & 6.SP.5	Spark 6.5	7.SP.1 & 7.SP.2	Spark 7.2

APPENDIX

B

Wii Games Used in Lesson Sparks

TABLE B.1 Which Wii Game by Grade

Grade	Lesson sparks using		
	Wii Sports	Wii Sports Resort	Wii Fit Plus
K	K.1, K.2	K.3, K.4	K.5, K.6
1	1.1, 1.2	1.3, 1.4	1.5, 1.6
2	2.1, 2.2	2.3, 2.4	2.5, 2.6
3	3.1, 3.2	3.3, 3.4	3.5, 3.6
4	4.1, 4.2	4.3, 4.4	4.5, 4.6
5	5.1, 5.2	5.3	5.4, 5.5, 5.6
6		6.1, 6.2, 6.3	6.4, 6.5, 6.6
7		7.1	7.2, 7.3, 7.4, 7.5, 7.6

TABLE B.2   Specific Wii Games Used in Lesson Sparks

Specific Wii game	Lesson sparks by grade		
	K–2	3–5	6–7 and GT*
Wii Sports			
Bowling	K.1 & K.2	4.1	
Golf		5.1	
Tennis		5.2	
Wii Sports Training			
Baseball: Hitting Home Runs	1.1		
Baseball: Batting Practice	2.2		
Baseball: Swing Control		3.1	
Bowling: Power Throws	1.2	3.2 & 4.2	
Golf: Target Practice	2.1		
Wii Sports Resort			
Air Sports: Skydiving	K.4		
Archery	1.3		
Basketball: 3-Point Contest		3.3	
Bowling: 100-Pin Game		5.3	6.3
Canoeing: Speed Challenge			6.2
Frisbee: Frisbee Dog		3.4	
Golf (3 Holes)			7.1
Swordplay: Speed Slice	K.3	4.3	6.1
Table Tennis: Table Tennis Return	1.4 & 2.4		
Wakeboarding	2.3	4.4	
Wii Fit Plus: *Aerobics*			
Hula Hoop	2.5		
Two-People Run		5.5	

TABLE B.2 *(Continued)*

Specific Wii game	Lesson sparks by grade		
	K–2	3–5	6–7 and GT*
Wii Fit Plus: *Balance Games*			
Balance Bubble			7.6
Penguin Slide	1.6	5.4	6.6
Ski Jump		3.5	6.5 & 7.2
Soccer Heading	K.6	3.6	6.4
Table Tilt	1.5		
Tightrope Walk	2.6		7.4
Wii Fit Plus: *Training Plus*			
Bird's-Eye Bull's-Eye			7.3
Driving Range		4.5	
Perfect 10	K.5		7.5
Snowball Fight		4.6	
Tilt City		5.6	

*GT. Gifted and talented students in Grades 4 and 5, ages 9 and up

APPENDIX

C

NETS (National Educational Technology Standards)

NETS for Students (NETS·S)

All K–12 students should be prepared to meet the following standards and performance indicators.

1. Creativity and Innovation

Students demonstrate creative thinking, construct knowledge, and develop innovative products and processes using technology. Students:

   a. apply existing knowledge to generate new ideas, products, or processes

   b. create original works as a means of personal or group expression

   c. use models and simulations to explore complex systems and issues

   d. identify trends and forecast possibilities

2. **Communication and Collaboration**

   Students use digital media and environments to communicate and work collaboratively, including at a distance, to support individual learning and contribute to the learning of others. Students:

   a. interact, collaborate, and publish with peers, experts, or others employing a variety of digital environments and media

   b. communicate information and ideas effectively to multiple audiences using a variety of media and formats

   c. develop cultural understanding and global awareness by engaging with learners of other cultures

   d. contribute to project teams to produce original works or solve problems

3. **Research and Information Fluency**

   Students apply digital tools to gather, evaluate, and use information. Students:

   a. plan strategies to guide inquiry

   b. locate, organize, analyze, evaluate, synthesize, and ethically use information from a variety of sources and media

   c. evaluate and select information sources and digital tools based on the appropriateness to specific tasks

   d. process data and report results

4. Critical Thinking, Problem Solving, and Decision Making

Students use critical-thinking skills to plan and conduct research, manage projects, solve problems, and make informed decisions using appropriate digital tools and resources. Students:

   a. identify and define authentic problems and significant questions for investigation

   b. plan and manage activities to develop a solution or complete a project

   c. collect and analyze data to identify solutions and make informed decisions

   d. use multiple processes and diverse perspectives to explore alternative solutions

5. Digital Citizenship

Students understand human, cultural, and societal issues related to technology and practice legal and ethical behavior. Students:

   a. advocate and practice the safe, legal, and responsible use of information and technology

   b. exhibit a positive attitude toward using technology that supports collaboration, learning, and productivity

   c. demonstrate personal responsibility for lifelong learning

   d. exhibit leadership for digital citizenship

6. Technology Operations and Concepts

Students demonstrate a sound understanding of technology concepts, systems, and operations. Students:

a. understand and use technology systems

b. select and use applications effectively and productively

c. troubleshoot systems and applications

d. transfer current knowledge to the learning of new technologies

NETS for Teachers (NETS·T)

All classroom teachers should be prepared to meet the following standards and performance indicators.

1. **Facilitate and Inspire Student Learning and Creativity**

   Teachers use their knowledge of subject matter, teaching and learning, and technology to facilitate experiences that advance student learning, creativity, and innovation in both face-to-face and virtual environments. Teachers:

   a. promote, support, and model creative and innovative thinking and inventiveness

   b. engage students in exploring real-world issues and solving authentic problems using digital tools and resources

   c. promote student reflection using collaborative tools to reveal and clarify students' conceptual understanding and thinking, planning, and creative processes

   d. model collaborative knowledge construction by engaging in learning with students, colleagues, and others in face-to-face and virtual environments

2. **Design and Develop Digital-Age Learning Experiences and Assessments**

   Teachers design, develop, and evaluate authentic learning experiences and assessments incorporating contemporary tools and resources to maximize content learning in context and to develop the knowledge, skills, and attitudes identified in the NETS·S. Teachers:

   a. design or adapt relevant learning experiences that incorporate digital tools and resources to promote student learning and creativity

b. develop technology-enriched learning environments that enable all students to pursue their individual curiosities and become active participants in setting their own educational goals, managing their own learning, and assessing their own progress

c. customize and personalize learning activities to address students' diverse learning styles, working strategies, and abilities using digital tools and resources

d. provide students with multiple and varied formative and summative assessments aligned with content and technology standards and use resulting data to inform learning and teaching

3. Model Digital-Age Work and Learning

Teachers exhibit knowledge, skills, and work processes representative of an innovative professional in a global and digital society. Teachers:

a. demonstrate fluency in technology systems and the transfer of current knowledge to new technologies and situations

b. collaborate with students, peers, parents, and community members using digital tools and resources to support student success and innovation

c. communicate relevant information and ideas effectively to students, parents, and peers using a variety of digital-age media and formats

d. model and facilitate effective use of current and emerging digital tools to locate, analyze, evaluate, and use information resources to support research and learning

4. Promote and Model Digital Citizenship and Responsibility

Teachers understand local and global societal issues and responsibilities in an evolving digital culture and exhibit legal and ethical behavior in their professional practices. Teachers:

    a. advocate, model, and teach safe, legal, and ethical use of digital information and technology, including respect for copyright, intellectual property, and the appropriate documentation of sources

    b. address the diverse needs of all learners by using learner-centered strategies and providing equitable access to appropriate digital tools and resources

    c. promote and model digital etiquette and responsible social interactions related to the use of technology and information

    d. develop and model cultural understanding and global awareness by engaging with colleagues and students of other cultures using digital-age communication and collaboration tools

5. Engage in Professional Growth and Leadership

Teachers continuously improve their professional practice, model lifelong learning, and exhibit leadership in their school and professional community by promoting and demonstrating the effective use of digital tools and resources. Teachers:

    a. participate in local and global learning communities to explore creative applications of technology to improve student learning

    b. exhibit leadership by demonstrating a vision of technology infusion, participating in shared decision making and community building, and developing the leadership and technology skills of others

    c. evaluate and reflect on current research and professional practice on a regular basis to make effective use of existing and emerging digital tools and resources in support of student learning

    d. contribute to the effectiveness, vitality, and self-renewal of the teaching profession and of their school and community